Robert Henry Newell

Studies in Stanzas

Robert Henry Newell

Studies in Stanzas

ISBN/EAN: 9783743303584

Manufactured in Europe, USA, Canada, Australia, Japa

Cover: Foto ©Thomas Meinert / pixelio.de

Manufactured and distributed by brebook publishing software (www.brebook.com)

Robert Henry Newell

Studies in Stanzas

STUDIES IN STANZAS

BY

ORPHEUS C. KERR

NEW YORK
THE USEFUL KNOWLEDGE PUBLISHING COMPANY
No. 18 Vesey Street
1882

CONTENTS.

TINTS OF THE TIMES.

	PAGE.
THE IMPERIAL VOTARESS	7
FAMILY READING	13
"SIMILIA SIMILIBUS CURANTUR."	16
FIAT JUSTITIA	23
GRANT	26
OWGOOST AND MAHREE	33
WATTS IN A PANIC	36
PLAY OF THE PERIOD	38
RECOGNITION	41
RECONSTRUCTED	45
THAT AWFUL DAD	50
WATCH CÆSARISM	54
SUMNER	58
NO SANTA CLAUS	61
A CUP TO CHRISTMAS	66
FRAUD BY HEAVEN	69
AT THE SPRINGS	71
THE BROKEN RACER	74
JUST THE TROUBLE	77
THE MAN THEY HANG	81
CERTAIN VERSES	83
THE RIVEN AEROSTAT	86
"PUTS" AND "CALLS"	91
AT EASTER	94
THE MUTE	96
HYGEIA IN THE SOUTH	99
THE TRIUMPH	101
VOX DEI	106

THE NINE	108
PRO PATRIA MORI	110
THE "LAST" MAN	112
EPITHALAMIUM	115
BROTHER BLATHERS	117
IN LENT	122
THE DEAD NAPOLEON	124
HUMOR'S ILIAD	127
THE JESTER'S BURIAL	130

BALLADS AND BROADSIDES.

A FABLE OF FINANCE	137
CONDENSED TRAGEDIES	144
THE COMMON LOT	146
THE COMIC CHRISTIAN CLERGYMAN	148
BALLOON BALLADS	154
Balloon Him of the Republic	154
Mose	155
Laus Thetis	158
Infatuosity	159
The Sainted Damosel	160
UNDERWRITEOUSNESS	163
THE BOSTON MAN	170
CHICKEN AND EGGS ARE OUT	173
THE TRUCKEE REGATTA	181
BILLIARDS	184
A STOOP TO CONQUER	186
THE POLISHED LEGAL GENTLEMAN	191
SQUIBS FOR "THE FOURTH"	199
THE THIRD TERMAGANT	202
THE SLEIGHING OF OLD	209
BEAUTY AND BOOTY	214

TINTS OF THE TIMES.

STUDIES IN STANZAS.

THE IMPERIAL VOTARESS.

When Cœlia, tireless in her urgent mission,
  On quiet Mrs. Domus made a call,
From what she viewed as woman's false position
  Was drawn her plea for aid to Women all.

A lonely spinster, with a future cheerless
  As were the loveless years she'd left behind,
Her heart, unmated, from neglect was fearless
  To crave for more than Love for womankind.

No weak disciple she, to dream and linger,
  Because with doubting others might be dumb;
But hers to cry, erect, with beck'ning finger:
  I lead the way, my Sisters!—will you come?

The kindly matron of the modest dwelling,
  Serene in simple comfort and content,
She saw as one her higher nature quelling
  'Neath Wrongs which, comprehended, she'd resent.

And, paling, flushing with the bold excitement
  Of Teaching that as Truth which was unsought,
She hastened onward in her fierce indictment
  Of those the Truth who helped not as they ought.

"I seek you, Madame," was her grim petition,
  "To ask for our Memorial your name,
As that of one whose Sex's recognition
  The less than other's Equal, is its shame!

"The idle, empty, listless dolls of fashion,
  The vain, bedizened puppets of the ball,
The slaves of what mankind exalt as Passion,
  May kiss the golden fetters of their thrall;

"But you, a woman, bred of higher feeling,
  And conscious of a soul immortal, too,
Were never born to spend a life in kneeling,
  If Man lifts not to equal stature, You!

"Let puling Love for love-sick children answer,
    And servile household duties for the drudge;
Not Man's time-serving poet and romancer,
    But Woman's self, was made for Woman's judge.

"No longer waiting on our master's pleasure,
    To take the power he gives to us, or pelf,
We claim the Right our own rewards to measure,
    And e'en to cast the Ballot with himself!"

The Matron, heeding all that had been spoken,
    From quiet meditation raised her head;
One moment kept the silence soft unbroken,
    And then, with look and smile peculiar, said:

"If painful seemeth my complete refusing
    Your Suffrage Right Memorial to sign,
Take consolation from my bolder choosing
    A far more daring method and design.

"While you are asking for the poor concession
    Of right to vote with Men, the same as they,
'Tis left for me, by slow and sure progression,
    To cast Two precious ballots in a day!"

As Cœlia, frowning, stood aloof and rigid,
  To hear her cause and calling made a jest,
One gentle look she caught—and was less frigid,
  And something mutely-tender stirred her breast.

A hand inviting mildly came to meet her,
  And, ere she could resist it, she was led
To where the vision, fairy-like, to greet her
  Was e'en a tiny morsel of a bed.

With silent touches dainty curtains lifted,
  As though their fleecy folding held a noise,
She saw, beyond the snowy portal rifted,
  In loving clasp asleep, Twin Baby-boys.

And, smiling fondly, spoke the happy mother:
  " In these, the Rights that Nature makes my own,
I live and rule the peer of Man, my brother,
  From humblest thatch of shelter, to the throne!

" He, kneeling knightly, in a love the purest,
  Was vassal to the Kingdom these should bring ;
Without them I were poorer than the poorest,
  And with them I am richer than a King!

"To Husband, Children, I as Woman loyal,
  Resign my own dominion of my life,
And they return it doubly told, and royal,
  In higher reign of Mother and of Wife.

"By fearless battle with the Right's offender,
  These Boys of ours their father's own shall seem;
By manly strength to man and woman tender,
  In gentler likeness l shall be supreme.

"The Natures mingling in a blest Communion,
  Ere yet their lives, its glory, were begun,
Shall dwell together in their brother union,
  To blend their parents, Equal, into One.

"If, growing grandly unto manhood's station,
  Their father's spotless honors theirs should be,
From all that makes them noble to the nation,
  Shall come a crown of glory unto Me.

"And when, the freeman's sov'reign moment reaching,
  Their Votes to purpose worthy they consign,
By all that holds them true to Mother-teaching,
  The Ballots they deposit shall be Mine!"

Thus speaking, softly, and with fervent feeling,
  Her eyes upon her darlings in their bed,
She saw not where the other forth was stealing,
  With downcast eyelids, too, and drooping head.

Oh, spirit fairer, and of subtler reason!
  Oh, Woman, first in Man's supremest grace!
His rule is but his loyalty or treason,
  To yours beside the cradle of our race.

FAMILY READING.

An American male parent, unto his babes said he:
"Come hither, pretty little ones, and sit on either knee,
And tell me what you've lately heard your mother read, and me?"

In his fatherly assurance, and fond, parental way,
He wanted to discover what the innocents would say
About the Missionary-book they'd heard the other day.

Full of glee spake young Alonzo, all legs and curly hair,
"You yead about the man they hung, and all the people there;
And mamma yead the funny part, of how it made him swear."

Joining quickly in, cried Minnie—all waist and
    dimpled neck:
"It wasn't half so funny, though, as that about
    the check
They caught somebody forging, 'cause he was so
    green, I 'speck."

"But the thing I liked the bestest," Alonzo piped
    amain,
"Was how somebody yunned away, and won't
    come back again,
And tookt somebody's wife with him upon a yail
    yoad train."

"Then you wasn't list'ning, 'Lonzo," came swift
    from Minnie, small,
"When papa read about the girl that tookt her
    only shawl,
And wrapt a baby up in it, and left it in a hall."

"Oh, I wa'n't, hey?" trilled Alonzo, dismayed to
    be outdone;
"I'm go'n' to learn to yead, myself; and you can
    have the *Sun*;
And I'll yead *Herald* 'Personals,' and never tell
    you one!"

The American male parent, his hair arose on end;
On either knee an infant form he did reverse and bend,
And from their little mouths straightway made dismal sounds ascend.

"SIMILIA SIMILIBUS CURANTUR."

Miss Dora Delaine, of West Livingston place—
A rose in her bloom and a lily in grace—
Fell sick, in an hour, of what none could define,
But wiseacres called going into decline.

It happened this way: on the night of the ball
To Russia's Grand Duke, young Alexis the tall,
While Music and Mirth, fairy twins as they are,
Were paying their court to the son of the Czar,
And lights sparkling endless, and jewels and
    flow'rs
Lent luster and hue to the wings of the hours,
Ere yet her proud eyes lost the fire of their
    glance,
Our Dora turned faint in a pause of the dance.

The heat, or the crowd, or excitement, 'twas said,
Thus made in a moment her cheeks like the dead;

And ices, and essences pungent, and fans
Were proffered, and fluttered; and various plans
Were hinted for gaining more air; but she sighed
The single word "Home!" and would not be denied.

Papa and mamma, when the carriage was called,
Bore homeward poor Dora, all muffled and shawled;
And not from that night was she ever the same
Bright spirit of health; but as languid and tame
And dull as a bird that refuses to sing,
And droops in his cage with his head in his wing.

At first it was thought the affection was slight,
Some freak of a chill, or of lacing too tight;
But when to her face there returned not its bloom,
And listless and pale she remained in her room,
The family doctor was summoned to see
Whatever the matter could possibly be.

To humor her mood—which was rather ill-bred—
He came as her friend, not physician, he said;

And, having first talked of the weather and news,
Remarked, that he feared Miss Delaine had "the blues,"
And hoped, for the sake of herself and her friends,
She'd take a prescription of tincture which tends
To fuse with its iron the blood, and give tone—
"O, pshaw!" exclaimed Dora, "do leave me alone!
I *hate* your old drugs!" and the pointed rebuff
Offended the doctor, who left in a huff.

Two other practitioners, stately and grave,
Appeared in their turns and their evidence gave:
"Digestive inertia," said one; "and for you
Some acid sulphuric, diluted, will do."
"It's nervous-pulmonic," the other observed;
"Take Jink's Hypo-phosphates, and don't be unnerved."
"I'm *well!*" Dora cried, in hysteric revulse—
"I *won't* show my tongue, and you *sha'n't* feel my pulse!"

Her father perplexed, between anger and pain,
Bethought him at last of young Doctor Migraine,—
Who came from the South, when the fighting was done,
To practice in Gotham, where fortunes are won,—
And, calling him in, laid a hand on his knee,
And said: "You will find, sir, my daughter to be
Convinced she is well, 'spite of all you can say;
Yet dwindling and peaking and pining away."

"I've heard of the case, and have seen Miss Delaine,
And went to the ball," answered Doctor Migraine;
Nor spoke any more till he entered the room
Where Dora was drooping in silence and gloom.

"A doctor, again!" was her sigh of despair—
"Oh, when will it end?" He selected a chair,
And, seating himself with his face to her own,
Replied: "You can tell that yourself, and alone!
My words shall be few, and as plain as my art;
You're sick, Miss Delaine, with disease of the heart."

'Twas rather the tone than the language that made
Miss Dora breathe quick, as she said, half afraid,
"Why, what can you mean?" He was swift to reply,
"That night, at the ball, very near you was I."

She stared and grew white, and the speaker went on :
"I can't say I saw, but I *heard* what was done;
One moment you beamed—('*But Montgomery Sill
'S engaged to 'Bel Vaughn*')—in the next you were ill!"

She started to rise, with the tears on her face—
"Your words are insulting!" He bowed from his place—
"One moment," he begged, "till I've said what I may;
Then chide, if you choose, and I'll hasten away.

"The words I o'erheard with yourself at the ball,
Are not more for me than for you to recall
With pride or delight—(if indeed you are still
Inclined to waste thought on Montgomery Sill);—

Similia Similibus Curantur.

For Isabel Vaughn, with a friend of my heart
Once played such a cruel, perfidious part,
That now, even now, when his care's at an end,
I feel, and am spurned, and betrayed with my friend!

"A guest from the South at the Springs, in a time
When fortune was his in his own sunny clime,
He bowed to her charms, nor resisted the spell
That urged him to woo her, the fair Isabel!
His suit was accepted; they parted, to meet
No more until war, like a tempest of sleet,
Had blighted his fortunes, with others, ah me!
When Sherman passed through on his March to the Sea.
And then, when he offered release, in his pride,
To her who had promised her hand as his bride,
She answered the note with this stab of the pen—
''Twas but a flirtation—'tis ages since then!'

"And now she is pledged to Montgomery Sill!
The friend of my heart, lives he under it still?
He does; and confides to Miss Dora Delaine
He shares her disease, and his name is Migraine!"

You see how it was: they were surely a pair,
This southron ill used, and the sorrowful fair;
And all that remains for a mortal to guess
This hint from a letter may briefly express:

"My friends in the South" (wrote the doctor one day),
"You know I'm an allopath, hot, in my way,
And that, hitherto, I've belonged to the school
Esteeming a rival a knave or a fool;
But, lately, I've had such a wonderful case,
That, sooner than lose it, I've dared the disgrace
Of making the point, beyond questioning, sure,
That like is for like an infallible cure!
My patient, the loveliest queen of a girl
That ever drew kings in the chain of a curl,
Was fading away with that exquisite smart
I'd carried for years in my own weary heart;
And after due visits, by no means for pelf,
For life I've prescribed—wish me joy in't!—myself!"

FIAT JUSTITIA.

Hand me here my cap and bells,
  Throw the motley o'er me;
Then from out the prison cells,
  Drag the wretch before me!
I'll, in public virtue's name,
  Bring him to repentance;
Make him feel a felon's shame,
  And pronounce his sentence.

Now, you villain! look at me,
  Hear my words consistent;
Yours the deadly sin we see,
  Lately, too persistent.
If you weep, 'tis guilt confessed,
  Worse than can be pardoned;
If you smile, the fact expressed,
  Is, that you are hardened.

Crime it was that made your crime—
  Say you—but its blackness
Finds no censure in a time
  Rank with moral slackness—
He you slew your all had stole?—
  Why, you simple noddy!
He would only kill a soul;
  You have killed a body.

If for that same first offense
  Life itself must answer,
Who'd be living one hour hence?
  Tell me, if you can, sir!
Possibly a saint or two,
  And the baby-creatures;
Few besides could 'scape the rue;
  No, not even preachers.

Tradesmen trade in weaker souls,
  Lovers pick and buy them,
Lawyers make them lie in scrolls,
  Judge and jury try them;

Priests prepare them for the flight
   Doctors do insure them,
All combine to seal their plight,
   None to guard and cure them.

He you slew would kill a soul?—
   Why, you simple noddy!
By that rule, upon the whole,
   You'd kill anybody.
Hanged be you, and then entombed,
   For your wicked capers—
Tried by whom—you ask—and doomed?
   By the daily papers!

GRANT.

"The King is dead—long live the King!" they clamor,
  When moves a Crown from falling head to high,
To throw o'er frail humanity a glamour,
  That, raised to Royalty, it cannot die.

The golden circlet, flaming gems of ages,
  By craven homage held in upper air
Eternal shines through long historic pages,
  A symboled stamp of godhead deathless there.

No fable ours, like this, to gild immortal
  The name and office first in peace and strife;
They are but men who pass our loftiest portal,
  And perish from it in the midst of life.

By deeds of honor, duty or demerit,
  They make their crowns, of pure or baser ore,
To wear what they of their own worth inherit,
  Or sink, all crownless, to be known no more.

To thee, our Soldier-President, returning
    Unto the ranks from seat supreme of sway,
What meed shall give thy Country as thine earning,
    When blinding partisanry fades away?

From clouds of War that thine own sword had riven;
    Ere yet thy head above their gloom was clear;
While rang for thee, or thee arraigned, to heaven
    Thy troopers' shouting and the widows' tear;

The great Republic summoned thee to station
    Made doubly great by thy victorious aid,
When through the blood-stained highways of the Nation
    The long-roll answered to the cannonade.

By battle's seething thunderbolt ignited,
    Columbia's natal planet earliest burned;
'Twas to the sword her virgin love was plighted,
    And to the sword the precious trust returned.

She called in no uncertain tones of heeding,
  That thou should'st bear thy laurels to the place
Where martyr blood of Mercy slain was pleading
  For justice panoplied in sterner grace.

A loyal Captain, trained to follow orders,
  A man to them obeying as to fate,
Thy marching answer took thee o'er the borders
  Between the camp-fire and the halls of state.

A Captain true, unused to Party's scheming,
  Nor deeper versed in wiles to meet its own,
As in the field for half-lost Fight's redeeming,
  In Faction's feud thou stood'st almost alone.

What marvel, then, that carping tongues assaulted
  The silent leader, open as the day;
That bold Vainglory thought the Chief had halted
  When firm he stood, a lion, in its way!

Where quailed the will at Donelson the victor;
  O'er Vicksburg's walls of steel and flame no less;
Inexorable the Republic's lictor,
  To bear her fasces through the Wilderness?

In War a bolt with no resounding thunder
  To cry the havoc of its dread release,
Thy plain, straight way, sententious to our wonder,
  A noiseless mastery, prevailed in Peace.

No word from lips inscrutable of omen,
  For good or evil, answered hatred's plea;
For friends thy hand, and for the conquered foeman
  A Brother-Soldier's tacit chivalry.

And fared the Land the worse for thine endeavor
  To fill with Acts unspoken Duty's part?
A modest hero she had known thee, ever,
  And for thy motives took thee to her heart.

The placeman's clangor rising to her hearing,
    From thee to tear the State's potential scroll,
Her voice responsive, mighty and unfearing,
    Again acclaimed thee at the Capitol.

Not thine the fault that made this added glory
    A prize attained through uncongenial strife,
With one long living the sublimest story
    To end, ignobly wiled, a noble life.

Alas! for him, the Scribe of simple manner,
    In zeal for failing fellow-mortal brave,
Lured from the grove to bear a periled banner,
    And find beneath its fated folds the grave.

Not yet the laurel knows the peaceful zero
    To bid the humbler bay above it bloom;
Still gives the court its honors to the hero,
    And to the sage derision and a tomb.

And better thus, despite untold complaining,
    The place for valor is the sov'reign seat,
There to be swift and mighty in maintaining
    The voice upraised by wisdom in the street.

To each its office, noble by contrasting;
   A grace of empire shared alike by each;
First in the van the man of action casting
   A shade, as shines, behind, the man of speech.

So trusted Twice, when Sage and Knave, combining,
   Had sought thy fall with threat and witless jibe,
And sophist Spleen had brought to thy defining
   The venal newsman's dastard diatribe;—

Let finger touch the record's line revealing
   One deed thine honor's conscience should atone;—
If friends were false, then thine the honest feeling,
   And theirs the sin that made the shame their own.

Thy hand had wrought full many a noble action,
   To hide what simple faith was erring there,
Had not the fell, ambitious mask of Faction,
   Turned stone before thee in the Senate's chair.

For peace to govern raised supreme o'er others,
  As erst a captain war's behest to fill;
Not of thyself a ruler of thy brothers:
  By trust of theirs a captain, only, still;—

In their approval mercifully binding
  The wounds an angry, erring brother knew;
Something in him to manhood loyal finding,
  That to his own, or right or wrong, was true;—

No gain thou had'st of wealth—save for thy
    Nation
  Of Gold to make her pledge and promise good;
Thou wentest forth from thankless cares of
    station,
  By thine own friends scarce justly understood.

But these the glories bringing fame upon thee
  In future years, in clearer majesty:
The patriot's truth, the soldier's might, that won
    thee
  The heart of Lincoln and the sword of Lee.

OWGOOST AND MAHREE.

On Newport sands, at eventide,
Walked youth and maiden side by side:
    She wore the latest,
        The latest style of dress;
    And he—in kids and tall white hat—
        Himself did thus express:
" Let me fan you; I'll fan you, my Mahree,
For scarcely comes a breath of air from off the beastly sea."

The stars, alone, their stroll did note,
And saw them reach a stranded boat;
    Soon she was seated,
        Was seated thereupon:
    But not before, unto herself,
        She thought of damage done—
" O, my panier! my panier, starched and shirred;
To sit upon a hateful boat is perfectly absurd!"

He fanned her brow, and sighed, and said:
" I wonder if your pa's abed?—

Say ain't it jolly,
　　So awful jolly, though,
　　To have him think you do not care
　　　A straw for me, you know!
But, how *can* you, how *can* you be so deuc'd
Unmoved at what's so deucid slow for me, your
　　own Owgoost?"

Upon the beach a gaiter neat,
In pretty petulance did beat;
　　Then she looked upward,
　　　Looked upward with a smile,
　　A lovely blush, unseen by him,
　　　Upon her face the while:
"Now, you man, you! you man, you!" cried
　　Mahree;
"How utterly ridiculous to say such things to
　　me!"

As thus they cooed upon the shore,
There came a sudden angry roar:
　　It was her father;
　　　Her father, the old man,
　　Who'd shuffled down from his hotel,
　　　The figures twain to scan.

Yes, to scan you, to scan you, loving pair;
And of his wrath do you, Mahree, and you,
    Owgoost, beware!

"That fellow make return your fan,
And come with me, Miss Mary Ann!
    Now you, get out, sir!
      Get out, Augustus Jones!
    Nor let me hear a word from you,
      If you would save your bones!
Have her? Dang ye! why dang ye for a fool!
You're on a salary, and she goes back to boarding school."

WATTS IN A PANIC.

O ENVY not the poor his pride,
  Though rich in stocks and bank thou art,
Nor deem the purse with naught inside
  Assureth a contented heart;
For ne'er to call a cent thine own
  Is but a mortal still to be,
And oft a sting of grief is known
  Unto the greatest penury.

Though in the flaunting pauper's lot,
  No mad'ning railroad shares intrude,
Although the unmoneyed mind is not
  With wild Trust Companies imbued;
Yet " North Pacific " unpossessed
  Can scarce for perfect peace avail,
And more is needed to be blessed
  Than not to know " Pacific Mail."

The ever impecunious soul,
   Without a penny to his name,
In jeering poverty may roll,
   And make thee wistful for the same,
While at his spirit's deepest core
   Exists, perchance, a sadder blank
Than if he owned thy hoarded store,
   And had it in a savings bank.

Then bear the sorrows of thy wealth
   With manly fortitude and tact;
"Northwestern" leaves thee yet thy health,
   And "Western Union" may react.
More ways to happiness there are
   Than not to be a dollar worth,
And "Erie" held to wait for par,
   Excelleth beggary from birth.

PLAY OF THE PERIOD.

The lingering, last orchestral swell
    Along the crowded lobbies drifted,
When, at the prompter's signal bell,
    The curtain from the stage was lifted;
And then, the flutter of applause
    Was not that favorite might be bolstered,
But murmured through the house because
    So finely was the scene upholstered.

A glowering husband strode and fumed,
    To think upon his wife unstable,
While she in pensive beauty bloomed
    Beside a really lovely table;
What time a certain young Alphonse,
    Whose flirting caused connubial cholers,
Stood leaning near a statue bronze,
    Worth, easily, a hundred dollars.

The general story seemed to be
   Of marriage that had been too hasty,
And ran its round of misery
   'Mongst chairs and sofas rich and tasty;
"I love you not!" the lady said;
   "And, knowing that, 'tis all you *can* know;"
Then from her husband's pleading fled,
   And fainted near the grand piano.

From this ensued a meeting grim,
   Between the husband and the lover,
Within a park of verdure prim,
   Where chaste settees were spread all over.
A bullet, planted in his face,
   Cut short Alphonse's life of honey,
And sprawled him by a marble vase
   That must have cost a mint of money.

When next appeared the lady fair,
   She was declining with consumption,
Upon a 'broidered lounge, so rare
   To guess its price would be presumption;

And when, at last, for love she died,
   With husband, priest and poodle near her,
The scene was greatly glorified
   By an imported, spacious mirror.

If such was not the plot exact,
   It seemed the meaning of the bathos,
And, judged by any sober fact,
   Had equal want of pith and pathos.
'Twas not in captious spirit rash
   That people grave, when come an end did,
Pronounced it most immoral trash ;—
   But then the furniture was splendid!

RECOGNITION.

To his Vassal wrote the king:
  When thy City's liegemen greet me,
One shall be amongst them there,
  Greatest of the great to meet me.
    Thou may'st know him by his air;
    *See **that** thou his place prepare!*

Through the city rang the words,
  By a thousand voices spoken:
"Loyal in our watch are we
  For the mighty comer's token;
    We shall know him when we see
    That unto us cometh he."

Thus, at every trumpet's sound,
  To the gates the people thundered:
Scanned the prince or priest that came
  With his lordly train, and wondered
    If 'twas he whose lofty fame
    Put the greatest still to shame?

Rode the viceroys of the land
   From afar into the City,
With a courtly following,
   Heroes mailed and scholars witty;
     Each of worth to tilt or sing,
     For a prize before the King.

"Greatest these of all the Great!"
   Swelled the peoples' loud hosanna;
"Greater mortals there are nought
   In the fane, or under banner.
     Who of them has highest caught
     Honor in our Monarch's thought?"

So the quest and question grew,
   In the maze of rival glory;
This the one, or that, alone,
   Chief of future song and story;
     Till the distant highway shone
     With the splendor of the Throne.

Panoplied in pomp sublime,
   Like the sun, our Monarch nears men;
Plain and mountain blaze and shine
   With his chariots and spearsmen.

Recognition.

Sound the trump and form the line;
Who the Greatest he'll divine!

As the sea to kiss the shore,
  Rolled the myriad loyal-hearted
Through the gates to meet the King,
  Where the hills and valley parted;
    Praise unto his name to bring,
    That should lift it like a wing.

He descendeth from his car,
  Where the lords and priests assemble·
Lo, the mighty meet his glance,
  In their haughty pride, and tremble:
    Like the glitter of a lance
    Is the look he turns askance.

Spake the Vassal in his fear,
  While his heart beat fast and faster:
"Of my province greatest are
  These, thy slaves, my Lord and Master,
    Whose the noblest natal star,
    Thou hast visioned from afar!"

From the princes turned the King,
  And, in wave of his example,
Back recoiled the City's host,
  In a heaving swirl and trample;
    Beating down a wanderer tossed
    On its violence, and lost.

Torn and trod by meanest heel,
  Of his own unknown, unknowing;
To behold the Greatest, led
  By the people in their going—
    O'er him bowed the King, and said:
    " He is here—and he is **dead!** ",

RECONSTRUCTED.

I have never seen a Southern woman who had been "reconstructed."—Jefferson Davis's Speech at White Sulphur Springs, Va., 1873.

INTO Possumleigh, South Carolina, renowned for secession,
  When ended a war that for bitterness challenged comparison,
Marched a federal force, with its colonel, in martial progression,
  To camp in the same, for indefinite time, as a garrison.

They were angrily viewed, on their entry, as all had expected,
  By those of the place who had suffered from battle's calamity;
But a woman it was their protection most fiercely rejected,
  And scorned to the last their commander's profession of amity.

She had solemnly vowed, at the sound of the earliest cannon,
  To hate, while she lived, ev'ry Northerner bearing a bayonet;
And declared, when the rampart of Southland no more had a man on,
  She'd mount it herself, and her life as a sacrifice lay on it!

With a terrible frown of disdain for the people around her—
  Who, after a while, took the regiment's company graciously—
And a sentiment still, than before, in its hatred profounder,
  She hurled at them all her satirical compliments spaciously:

"You may loyally cringe in the dust to your merciful masters,
  And Yankees receive in the homes they have rendered deplorable,

But a womanly soul rises prouder from honor's
    disasters ;
  No country have I where the foe we have
    fought is adorable!"

To some family friends in the North, in a city of
    fashion,
  She fled, as she spoke, from her home and her
    kindred, indignantly ;
And they heartily gave her a welcome, in spite
    of her passion,
  Nor otherwise took her excusable wrath than
    benignantly.

In a drapery homespun and sober, she came on
    her visit ;
  A bonnet that seemed of the style of the Plio-
    cene period ;
And her beautiful hair, having no one to fix or
    to friz it,
  Was gathered as though it belonged to the
    head of a Nereid.

With a wonderful sense of the means that were fitted to soften
  A feminine soul in a frenzy of anger political,
Did her hostesses take her to seamstress and milliner often,
  And tempt her to give to the same her attention most critical.

Not a period tedious elapsed e'er she visibly brightened,
  And questioned the cost of each dainty and sumptuous article;
At the old-fashioned things she had on was unspeakably frightened,
  And showed of her lately resentful disdain not a particle;—

Till it certainly seemed that her anger was dying within her,
  As, changing her robes and her bonnet for those more Parisian-like,
It was morally plain that her temper grew weaker and thinner,
  And scorn of the North found her lips prone to meek indecision-like.

So the marvelous turn in her feelings went on through the season,
  The latest of styles being balm to her bosom's avidity ;
While the enmity cherished so lately, and scoffing at reason,
  Gave place unto love, with astonishing lightning rapidity.

And when, finally, home to the Southland her wardrobe she carried—
  The silks she had bought, and the bonnet so jaunty and blossomly,
It was, probably, dressed in the same that she presently married
  The colonel commanding the garrison at Possumleigh.

THAT AWFUL DAD.

TIME—*Noon.* SCENE—*A gorgeous morning room.*

Enter EXEMPLARY SON, *with a bottle of Vichy in one hand, and a goblet in the other.*

SON.

UPON my word, I'm only half awake,
And so this flashy, trashy stuff must take.
Oh, my poor head! it's quite as big again
As that which I in church reveal to men;
And I'm so thirsty!—really this must stop,
For of wild-oats I've reaped an overcrop.
Instead of staying out o' nights, begad!
I ought, at times, to stay at home with dad,
Or else, I fear, it's more than ten to one
He will forget he ever had a son.

Enter NURSE.

Well, nurse, how now! You've doubtless come to say
My father 'd like to bid me a good-day.

Make some excuse, while I to breakfast get—
I'm hardly fit, you know, to see him yet.
He's dressed, of course, and had his breakfast, too,
And gone his morning walk with Jane and you.
I hope my orders you see fit to mark,
That when you wheel him up around the park,
You let him not with other old men play,
Unless their nurses are with them to stay.
If in bad company he chance to fall,
I'll have to blame you, mistress, for it all.

NURSE.

Oh, sir, he's mostly just as good as gold;
I never saw a better man that old;
He scarcely gives a whimper or a pout,
Though two more teeth of his have just come out.
But, then, old men must be old men, they say:
And I surprised him only yesterday,
At work with heaps of paper and a quill,
And—would you believe me, sir?—he'd made his will!

SON.

His WILL! oh, horror! Nurse, can this be so?
Go bring him instant hither. Woman, go!

[*Exit* NURSE, *precipitately.*

Am I awake? His will! Well, I declare,
What next will fashionable fathers dare!
My sisters ought to be with him more strict,
Instead of being thus so derelict!
This comes because to whipping they're averse,
The old man's left to servants and the nurse;
No wonder, then, he does as he may please,
Makes wills, and chooses his own legatees.
I'll stop it, though, from this hour forth, if I
Have need the rod, in person, to apply.

Enter NURSE, *wildly agitated.*

Well, nurse, you've brought him, surely, have you not?

NURSE.

Oh, sir, if you'll believe the turn I've got!
I went to find the dear old creature, straight,
And he'd slipped out the open airy gate.
I followed after, quick as I could run,
And—oh, good lordy!—what d'you think he'd done?

SON.

Not gone to sell his bonds, or to dispose
Of real estate?—Speak! speak! my reason goes!

Nurse.

Much worse than that! Oh, sir, be calm, I pray,
Or I can't tell you what I have to say;—
The next-door's butler—which his name is Jack—
Beheld your father jump into a hack
Beside a lady dressed in silk and fur,
And—thinks he's run away to marry her!

Son (*tearing his hair*).

Blue blood and brimstone! Thunderationment!!
Arouse the house, and let the vale be rent!
Cry madness! murder! lunacy! and law!
Call out the press, and bid it wag its jaw!
A father weds without consent of son!
I'm cheated, crushed, deserted, and undone!

Knocks down the nurse; smashes all the furniture; tears out of the house; and immediately consults his lawyers as to the feasibility of the breakage of wills and the issuance of writs de lunatico inquirendo.

WATCH CÆSARISM.

Our friend, old Mr. Beat, was dead;
   We walked behind his bier,
And softly to each other said:—
A land its pride, a home its head,
   Lament together here.

No errors of his own had he,
   Or he himself belied;
But faults in others he could see,
And grief for man's iniquity
   Was that of which he died.

Beside me, clad in decent black,
   With grave and cleric air,
There moved a man who sighed "Alack!
What mortal power shall bring him back,
   To comfort my despair?"

Watch Cæsarism.

"He was my perfect moral twin,
  In wailing virtue's fall:
And saw the age we're living in
Is wholly given up to sin,
  And bitterness and gall.

"Like him I weep to see the day"—
  (He sighed it with a sob),
"When those we've trusted go astray
From out the straight and narrow way,
  And justice is a job.

"Behold our hapless native land,
  To ruin given o'er;
If Credit Mobilier we stand,
With back-pay clinging to his hand,
  The statesman's pure no more.

"Thus, ever since the war, has been
  The nation's swift decline;
In man nor woman can be seen
The honor, innocence, I ween,
  Of simpler auld lang syne.

"Each day some plundering scheme's begun,
　　Since battle flags were furled,
For earliest issue of the *Sun*,
And *Tribune's* rather later one,
　　And, latest, for the *World*.

"The very air is full of crime,
　　Corruption stalks abroad;
The good old Democratic time
Held no Ben Butler in its prime,
　　Nor any kind of fraud.

"But, oh! my friend"—and here he fell
　　Upon my neck with groans,
"Our direst woe is yet to tell—
Who reads the *Herald* knows it well,
　　And feels it in his bones—

"The people in their folly tame,
　　Will wake at last to rue
The great republic's crowning shame,
And *Cæsarism* is its name! * * *
　　It breaks my heart. * * * Adieu!"

Watch Cæsarism.

He leaves me, in a headlong flight,
  His face of tears a blotch ;
O, soul of peerless moral height !
Why pass thus fleetly from my sight?—
  Law bless me—where's my watch !

SUMNER.

March 11, 1874.

HE passes silent to his peers
   In that still chamber, dim and vast,
Where sit, invincible of years,
   The uncrowned monarchs of the past;
A grander embassy to know,
   In that far country overhead,
Than soul inheriteth below
   The white-robed senate of the dead.

In pageant eloquent of grief,
   A mourning nation at his tomb
But see a phantom of the chief,
   Through life's last mystery of gloom;
Another added unto those,
   For the great battle's shadow born,
Who feel, unguerdoned by the rose,
   The mortal anguish of the thorn.

A mighty memory has gone
   From the full volume of the hour,
The less a majesty passed on
   Than something measureless of pow'r;
A spirit missing from the page
   That yet incarnateth the song;
A presence parted from the stage,
   Though moves the drama still along.

The lighted beacon of his soul
   Shone o'er the billows chill and dark,
When freedom, fainting for a goal,
   In storm and thunder sought the ark;
And, paling gently in the ray
   Of peaceful morning from afar,
Was lost ineffable in day,
   To glow eternal as a star.

His country, bowing at his grave,
   Can yield a tender thought of grace
To him, impassionate, who gave
   The blow that sanctified his face;

Studies in Stanzas.

But, well remembering the zeal
  Wherewith he bore a bitter part,
Must yet heroically feel
  The blow that quivers in her heart

NO SANTA CLAUS.

A CURLY-HEADED trouble-house,
  Scarce higher than a chair,
With such a look of thoughtfulness
  As children often wear,
Upturned a chubby face and said,
  Beside his father's knee—
"If I am good, will Santa Claus
  Bring pretty things to me?"

The father, a philosopher,
  And skeptic overmuch;
Believing not in anything
  He couldn't see and touch;
Concluded that the time had come
  To make his boy as wise,
And teach him to discredit all
  He saw not with his eyes.

"There is no Santa Claus at all,
   My little man," he said,
"And they're but false and foolish tales,
   That put him in your head;
For, whether Christmas finds you good,
   Or bad as you can be,
No toyman down the chimney'll come,
   Nor ever yet did he."

The youngster clasped his tiny hands,
   "No Santa Claus!" he cried;
And drew away, and caught his breath,
   And not to whimper tried;
"No kind old Santa Claus at all,
   To come on Christmas Eve,
And if a little boy's been good,
   Some drums and things to leave?'

The philosophic sire explained
   How that was all a myth,
Which only meant some parent Brown,
   Or White, or Jones, or Smith;

No Santa Claus.

And how the fabled children's friend,
    To punish or delight,
Was but papa, or mother, here,
    On this and ev'ry night.

"No Santa Claus!" again the child,
    With drooping head, exclaimed,
And farther still drew back, as though
    Both frightened and ashamed;
Then dropped the precious, battered toy,
    He'd treasured for a year,
And frowned, as little children will,
    When they would hide a tear.

"Now go, be put to bed, my lad,
    'Tis past your hour, you know."
The boy, impatient, cried "I won't!"
    And temper such did show,
That soon the philosophic sire,
    As ne'er before he'd done,
Chastised into obedience
    His now rebellious son,

"That you, who've been so good before,
  Should act like this," cried he,
"Is strange enough to make me doubt
  That you the same can be!"
To which the little one replied,
  As sullenly he stood:
"You say there is no Santa Claus,—
  And why should I be good?"

At later hour there came a smoke
  From out the nursery door,
And thither all the household flew,
  From ev'ry startled floor.
Beside a blazing curtain they
  The little imp did catch—
"It's cause I have been whipped," said he,
  "I did it with a match!"

"He's bad enough to burn us all
  Alive, I do believe!"
The father cried, scarce knowing but
  His senses did deceive.

No Santa Claus.

For which the child, still sullenly,
 This single answer had:
" You said there was no Santa Claus—
 Why shouldn't I be bad?"

A CUP TO CHRISTMAS.

MERRY CHRISTMAS is here, with a smile and a
    cheer;
  Let all your old troubles and quarrels be ended!
For the friend that is near brew the punch and
    draw beer,
  And pledge a good wish to the foe who's
    offended.
      Though with him was the spite,
      And with you is the right,
  In bumper to bumper forgive him to-night;
For whoever makes plea 'neath the evergreen
    tree,
A prince of good fellows and welcome is he!

In our lot may be loss of the life-gilding dross,
  That rusts, or is bright, in the hold free, or
    grasping;
And perchance the green moss on the church-
    yard's pale cross,
  Is wet with our tears for a loved hand's lost
    clasping;

And the Old Year has said,
As he bowed his white head:
Absolve me! I took them—your gold and your
dead!
Let his soft answer be, 'neath the evergreen tree:
Our blessing, with Christmas, is given to thee!

There's a face fairer grows o'er the virginal
snows,
That wrap from the blast a young pilgrim and
stranger,
In the eyes a sweet light, as of Bethlehem's night
When worshiped the stars at a birth in a
manger;
It is Time's Latest Born,
In the flush of a morn,
That brings, as we serve him, the palm or the
thorn!
And our first loyalty, 'neath the evergreen tree,
A fireside and feast for his poor ones shall be!

Then desert not the strain till it rises again,
And echoes in gladness from floor unto rafter;

While the heart's lightest mood thanks the Giver
 of good,
 His praises arise in its music and laughter.
  And the goblet'fill high,
  And the toast we'll drain dry :
 Long life to what's noblest all under the sky !
For so reads the decree 'neath the evergreen
 tree,
Of old father Christmas, whose children are we !

FRAUD BY HEAVEN.

'Squire Mullet ever strove to show
    Of all things he possessed a smattering—
And taught opposing minds to know
    Their folly had no kind of mattering;
Nor did he find in all his path
    A rival to dispute his victory,
Till Parson Smith aroused his wrath,
    By stubborn logic contradictory.

The village with their warfare rang—
    Or, rather, with the squire's exuberance,
And tongues, in fierce-opposing clang,
    Inflamed each nose to red protuberance:
" I think 'tis so," the parson cries,
    " From all that I can comprehend of it."
" *I* know it's not," the squire replies—
    " I *know*, you know, and that's the end of it!"

The clashing twain, at certain date,
　　Agreed, by way of test-sagacity,
The next eclipse to calculate,
　　And digits give the moon's opacity.
By tables long the parson gave
　　Nine digits to the orb's obscurity:
Whereat the squire, with pompous wave,
　　Declared for eight he'd give security.

Arrived the night, and lo, the moon
　　Of digits showed that nine had darkening,
Which brought the parson, boastful, soon,
　　To vex the squire's indignant hearkening:
" You'll own you're wrong, sir ? "
　　　　　　　　" No, not I ! "
" To digits eight mistaken laud you lent."
" I'll never own it ! "
　　　　　　　　" No ?—and why ? "
" Because, sir, the excess is fraudulent ! '

AT THE SPRINGS.

Parent of the Period Loquitor.

"—And might have done better."—my daughter,
    you mean?
Why, that, my old crony, remains to be seen;
You speak with the freedom of friendship, you
    say,
And I will respond in a similar way.

As brotherly chums in our bachelor lives,
We came to the Springs on a skirmish for wives,
As partners in trade many summers we came,
And now, as old boys, we are hither the same.

So, let us talk frankly of things as they are:
You think my Augusta superior, far,
To him who returned from the ride to the lake,
Her suitor accepted, my blessing to take.

Young Jenkins has many a lovable trait,
And income enough from his father's estate;

He followed us here with his heart in his hand,
A suppliant more than my girl could withstand.

I'll own he's not brilliant; nor equals, perhaps,
The average run of society chaps;
And halts in a sentence, to think of a word,
Till ev'ry one pities, or votes him absurd.

Augusta, you say, has an intellect quick,
That never was given to mate with a stick;
A mind ever tuned to the loftiest strains,
And worthy at least of a husband of brains.

It all may be true of my daughter, my friend;
But how would you manage the matter to mend?
Constrained by no edict of pride or of pelf,
The choice you deplore she has made for herself.

A belle of three seasons, she finally brings,
To Newport at first, and at last to the Springs,
A fancy untouched by the wooing of wit,
To yield when a Jenkins lays siege unto it.

She's had men of intellect round her by scores,
The gallant and sprightly, as well as the bores;

But none made the venture; from which I infer,
She didn't want them, and they didn't want her.

I tell you, old partner, it's rubbish to preach
Of values unbalanced, where each selects each ;
Unmatched as they seem to the casual eye,
They mate by the law of demand and supply.

My daughter I love, as you very well know,
And wouldn't be likely to rate her too low,
But as for the merit o'er Jenkins you sing—
A woman is worth simply what she will bring.

THE BROKEN RACER.

YE thousands of the lofty stand,
    Prolong the mighty cheer,
That in the cloud of dust at hand,
    And thunder rolling near,
The beaten red and blue is seen
Behind the orange and the green!

Let peals of exultation strain
    The autumn's airy cup,
As through the golden-hazed champagne
    The bubbled beads spring up;
For, in embattled flight to-day,
The Favorite bears the prize away!

But here and there amid your throng,
    Are hearts to pity moved,
For him, the Chestnut winner long,
    To Bay the loser proved;
Remembering when his royal place
Was ever foremost in the race.

The Broken Racer.

How rang your plaudits to the sky
   When he, the whirlwind's son,
At speed that shook the earth swept by
   The mane of Leamington;
And now, above his drooping crest,
That faded glory is a jest.

Thus, when before assembled Rome
   The gladiator reeled.
And he, whose arm had oft struck home,
   Was prone upon the field,
The voices of his early fame
To death renounced him for his shame!

The glory of the victor's strength,
   Is his, alas! no more,
And fresher sinews come, at length,
   To pass him at the score;
And whip and spur are plied in vain,
He'll never be himself again!

Then lead him to his stable back,
   Without a word's caress;
The racer, fallen to a hack,
   Than hack itself is less;

Once having won a name the first,
To lose is to be twice accurst.

Not e'en the lackey of his stall,
   Shall yield at pity's touch,
And be the gentler to his fall
   In pondering how much
To him who fails is added sting,
That he was yesterday a king.

The honors of a mighty past
   Are lost to present proof,
When broken is his heart at last,
   And laggard is his hoof;
The fallen racer had his day,
And passes with its light away.

JUST THE TROUBLE.

With wild hair hanging about her ears
  And neck;
With fair brow wrinkled, her angry tears
  To check;
With curl and quiver contending round
  Her mouth;
She cometh, her Uncle Sam to sound,—
  The South,

" You think, I reckon, that I'll forget
  The way,
I've been maltreated by all your set,
  Some day;
You think I mind whatever you do,
  Or don't;
But as for saying how far that's true—
  I won't!

" You think I'm pouting, and must be snubbed,
  Because
I'll not take kindly to what you've dubbed
  Free laws,
Whereby my servants are so bereft
  Of tone,—
When all I ask is just to be left
  Alone!

" You think to bring me, from being the best,
  To least,
Of all your nieces, the North, the West,
  And East,
By setting above me inferiors once
  I ruled;
But soon'll be finding yourself a dunce—
  And fooled!

" You think by manner despotic, or
  Neglect,
To make me seem too Quixotic for
  Respect;

Yet I can stand it as long as you please,
    My man,
And leave you to take what victor's ease
    You can!

"You think"—but paused at look from her Uncle Sam,
That bore, in its blent surprise and fun,
    No sham;
"To tell you the truth, my niece; since here
    You call;
I've not been thinking of you, my dear,
    At all!"

THE MAN THEY HANG.

My dad and mammy drank until
   It ended in a fight;
But all his pounding didn't kill,
   For I was born that night.

And just about the minute same
   That saw me try to creep,
In boss's barn a pup there came
   Of dogs that hunted sheep.

They used to say my brother was
   The boss's little beast;
And we were called the twins, because
   Our ages matched at least.

I played with him, and he with me,
   Till he began to show
A taste for mutton, rather free,
   And then he had to go.

The Man they Hang.

That is, he had to go and wear
    A chain, by day and night,
Because the boss he couldn't bear
    To drown the pup outright.

"The fault is in his blood," he said,
    "And it would be a shame
To knock the creature on the head,
    When he is not to blame!

"It's only Christian duty, too,
    The beast to watch and keep;
Since, long before his birth, we knew
    His breed would slaughter sheep."

And so they kenneled him at last,
    And kept him fed and tied;
And had me from the dooryard cast,
    Because I stamped and cried.

"Be off, you little vagabond;
    Nor come again!" said they;
"Your temper's what your father owned;
    You'll finely end, some day!"

Soon after, dad and mammy went
    The way of drinking kind;
An awful spree—two pokers bent—
    And I was left behind.

It took not long for all to rage
    Against me, and they flung
These words at me: "By parentage
    You're born but to be hung!"

And that was so. By casting out,
    And casting out again,
I've come by murder's reddest route,
    To this black prison-den.

Well, dad and mammy ill-begot,
    My hanging-day is set!
I wonder if that dog's been shot,
    Or if they chain him yet?

CERTAIN VERSES

In anticipation of an absurd proposition that a Mr. Knickerbocker should, some day, be nominated for office in New York.

If gravely the proposal's made,
   And to himself referred it be,
From what he knows, I'm much afraid,
   He'll deem it an absurdity;
Before the gifts of public place,
   And pomps official, share he can,
He must exchange his native race,—
   He's only an American.

Our democratic government,
   With universal suffraging,
Cannot to such as he be lent,
   Without prodigious huff raging:
For notice unto Irving Hall,
   Or Tammany, repair he can,
And find they give him none at all—
   He's only an American.

Between the hosts a Kelly leads,
   And those of Ottendorfer class,
But little grace, howe'er he pleads,
   The Knickerbocker's offer has;
Humiliation, swift and tart,
   Himself and kindred spare he can,
By realizing at the start,
   He's only an American.

As independent candidate
   What laurels could he cull, again,
Opposing, say, a Brennan "slate,"
   A Conner, Walsh, or Mulligan?
Secure a shadow of support
   From journalism ne'er he can,
When, 'stead of Celt or German sort,
   He's only an American.

Depending on his moral worth,
   If, yet, he'll make a fight of it,
What hope is his, upon the earth,
   Of office, or a sight of it?

No native can bring out the vote
　A gentleman from Kerry can ;
His ticket has no kind of note—
　He's only an American.

You can't persuade to seek the polls—
　Or think the moment fit is, when
His city calls—that best of souls,
　The home-born Yankee citizen :
'Tis but when all the nation goes,
　Find leisure to be there he can,
And never else—which merely shows
　He's only an American.2

Wherefrom it seems, that in New York,
　The veriest of mockeries—
As though in Bremen or in Cork—
　To run a Knickerbocker is :
Not being either Pat or Hans,
　'Tis simply, in despair, he can
Confess what forfeits all his chance—
　He's only an American !

THE RIVEN AEROSTAT.

Through all the land what sounding fame was
    that
Which voiced the wonders of an aerostat,
With mighty leap to spurn the world we tread,
And sail the trackless distance overhead;
To seek the airy current of the sky
That ever eastward belts the azure high,
And on the pinions of the tempest glide
Above the ocean, to its farther side!

The very mention of the deed was fraught
With something potent of a godlike thought,
And stirred the mind, by soaring fancy won,
To gage what might be, by what had been,
    done.
Full oft the sphere by wings of ether borne
Had sought the zenith, like the sun of morn,
And, dwindling buoyantly, been lost to view,
In lesser voyage through the realms of blue.

The Riven Aerostat.

Before Columbus crossed the western main,
What fleets had sailed the nearer seas from Spain;
And who of all from Europe's coast that went,
But might, like him, have found a continent?
It was the daring of a soul and will
Beyond his time, that gave him faith and skill
To start as others, but the farther go,
And from their knowledge learn the more to know.

Why, then, impossible the airy flight,
From hours extended unto day and night;
From petty journey in the high expanse,
To sight of England or the coast of France?
The pow'r was there, and needed but the man
Its might to measure in a nobler span;
To do the better what was done before,
And by the much attained attain the more.

Thus all the land was filled with loud acclaim,
And thronging thousands to the pageant came,
When from the earth should slip its girded hold
The globe translucent on its venture bold,

And mount like night above the setting sun,
To course the stars until the race was won,
To gain the goal; or, e'en if blown astray,
For others, coming after, show the way.

As through the folds the subtle spirit flies,
To mold the body and to bid it rise,
Each heart beats faster with a strange delight,
And eyes flash brighter at the wondrous sight.
From the low ground a giant form upwells,
And to a dome of stateliest arching swells,
Which, rising swifter as the moments pass,
Looms like a golden temple o'er the grass.

It rounds the more, as mounting vapors urge,
Till, like vast planet on the heaven's verge,
Its poise majestic hides the day from view,
Save where a glow that seems its own streams
      through;
And, spreading grander to the autumn wind,
As though impatient thus to lag behind,
Strains at the bonds that hold its glory down,
And rolls in rustling air its lofty crown.

The Riven Aerostat.

Almost the act creative is complete;
Almost the splendid fabric springs to meet
The clouds that scud along the ocean track,
To lap its beauties in their fleecy rack:
When, with supremest effort to be free,
In one fierce burst to be, or not to be,
It flutters, pants, is rended, to a shout—
A vision ended, and a light blown out!

As at the crisis of some mighty part,
Of its own passion breaks the actor's heart;
As through a mortal tenement of clay
The soul too mighty finds by death its way:
What erst aspired to reach the starry heights,
Through days of toiling and through vigiled
    nights,
By its own spirit torn and downward cast,
Sank to the earth a lifeless wreck at last.

Let those who late the brave attempt approved,
To sneering pity of the fall be moved,
And say to others of their specious ilk:
The thing was cotton when it should be silk.

Thus ever that which garb the humblest wears,
More than the soul in dainty texture dares;
Thus when its failure shows a strength unthought,
The fate of Fustian is the lesson caught!

But once a thought of deed sublime conceived,
It grows by failures still to be retrieved;
If in one form too great of act to live,
Unto another it can potence give.
Made strong by knowing what its strength can bear,
And braver, learning what it has to dare,
Its final fruits its promises transcend,
And vindicate its genius in the end.

So though, by energy inspired too well,
Within the hour of victory it fell;
Though through the wound along its riven side
Rushed forth the soaring spirit of its pride;
The grand idea visioned in its birth
Lives yet to teach its kind to spurn the earth;
And to the loftiest current of the skies,
At last the ocean-aerostat shall rise!

"PUTS" AND "CALLS."

A WALL STREET IDYL.

FOR six fair years, good wife of mine,
    The world as married folks has known us,
Since first I Put my lips to thine,
    And gave to thee a ring as Bonus.
It scarcely seems so distant now,
    And yet our ages show it, certes;
A matronly Five-Twenty, thou,
    And I'm amongst the Seven-Thirties.

Perchance when thou, with soothing air,
    Hast called me "Duck!" I've been a lame one;
Or when thy mother styled me "Bear!"
    I've been a Bull—though quite a tame one;
But if one's Shares of good intent
    Are not what he is always large in,
At least I'm sure I never meant
    That mine should have too small a Margin.

If e'er that I was Short in Stock
    Of patience, thou hast been a mourner:
Or I'd a Check from thee, to lock
    My warmest feelings in a Corner,
Exchange of Notes on the above
    Has quickly sped the mood disgusted,
And left us Long in Bonds of love,
    With all our Diff'rences Adjusted.

Nor need I fear to ask, of right,
    What in our Days of Grace was proffered,
That thou should'st not Protest at Sight
    Of poverty, if Draught were offered;
Thy promise then to bear with all
    The chills of fate without a shiver,
In Fixed Security I Call
    Its Verbal Contract to Deliver.

That by a turn of fortune's wheel,
    I'm poorer than a young mechanic,
Is but enough to make us feel,
    I'm sure, but merest passing Panic;

And if we can no longer dress
  In cloth and silk of costly tissue,
We'll have our children still to bless,
  Nor ever deem them Over-Issue.

Beyond the city's crowded ranks,
  In humbler home and lesser striving,
A hearty Run upon the Banks
  May bring our early youth's reviving;
And if the future of my life
  Should be the present cloud's revoker,
I'll charge it to the dearest Wife
  That ever blessed a Broken Broker.

Studies in Stanzas.

AT EASTER.

In Lent's last twilight lulled to sleep
   By soft cathedral bells,
While yet upon the April air
   The solemn organ swells,
Her thoughts go out in vestal dreams
   To greet the Easter day,
As buoyant as the birds of dawn.
   And innocent as they.

The cadence of the hymn is lost
   In prima donna's trill,
That mingles with the merry note
   Of polka and quadrille;
And where but now the priest and choir
   Intoned the doom of wrong,
The strains of Offenbach inspire
   The fantasies of song.

At Easter.

No longer draped in mournful serge
   For man's repented guiles,
The altar of the brightening church
   Entwined with lilies smiles;
While through the sacred portal throngs
   A bridal train more fair
Than ever saw, with waking eyes,
   The girlish dreamer there.

Then o'er the broadening summer-land
   Of forest, field and stream,
The lover's-walk, the archery,
   The dancing sail agleam;
Her maiden fancy wings its way,
   Sweets sipping as it goes,
Herself spring's sweetest violet,
   And summer's fairest rose.

THE MUTE.

Four kindred Spirits stood around a grave
   Wherefrom the dark, dissevered mourner-train
   Had slow recoiled into the world again,
Like parted cable lapsing in the wave.

One touched the headstone lightly as a cloud;
   And One upon the right hand faced the Third,
   Who, on the left, trod softly as a bird;
The Last, unmoving, at the feet was bowed.

From all a golden light of life was cast;—
   A soft, transcendent luster of the eye,
   The subtle glory native to the sky;—
From all save her, the bowed, unmoving Last.

She at the tablet-marble of the head
   A gleaming trump and scroll of parchment bore;
   She on the right the sword and balance wore:
A spotless shield before the Third was spread;

The Mute.

But for the bending Spirit at the feet,
   In robes of sable clad and drooping veil,
   No emblem gracious shone to tell the tale
Of lofty mission from a life complete.

" Hence swiftly flying from his grave," said Fame,
   " 'Tis mine to trumpet over all the earth
   The life-ennobling story of his worth,
And write the deathless honors of his name ! "

" And mine," said Justice, " e'er to follow thee,
   That naught o'ertold the final truth defile ;"
   " And mine," said Mercy, " both to reconcile ;
And to the Fourth, unmoving, turned the Three.

" Oh thou, our sister, motionless and mute !
   For us who speech and scroll of memory gave ;
   Thou bride of Death and angel of the Grave,
Of mortal growth to God the sweetest fruit—

" We leave thee watching, where no others are,
   In sable draped that we may whiter shine ;
   All that we are is lesser grace than thine,
And thou the cloud that folds our natal star ! "

Then upward winging through the ether, fleet,
   With arms enclasped, arose the shining Three;
   But ever, fading, looking back to thee,
Thou Shade Eternal, bowing at the feet.3

For thou art Silence; hiding in thy breast
   The all that to the shadows of the tomb
   Might give a deeper barrier of gloom,
And move the world's dead anchors to unrest.

HYGEIA IN THE SOUTH.

Extract from a private letter.

" HEED not, my friend, the foolish tales you hear
   Of Southern sickness in this summer season;
They're based on idlest rumors, far and near,
   Without a particle of truth or reason.
Like all the world we have our heated term,
   When vital vigor less, in some degree, grows,
But this involves no dread disease's germ,
      Except for negroes.

" The fevers few, that come with rainy spring,
   And into later periods have extension,
Are rarely, I assure you, anything
   That can't be shunned by very slight attention.
Perhaps the stranger feels a little ill,
   If he with fruit and evening air too free grows;
But they whom these malarial trifles kill,
      Are chiefly negroes.

"It may be true, the Asiatic scourge
   Is more or less with us until October;
But mild it is, to merest meagrim's verge,
   To those whose living, for a time, is sober.
It works its worst where first it did arrive,
   In town that by the river or the sea grows;
Yet even there, the ones who don't survive,
       Are mainly negroes.

"Aside from spinal troubles, now and then,
   And qualms dyspeptic, feasts to put a check on,
We, Southern people—children, dames and men,
   Are healthier far than many Yanks, I reckon.
Our servile class will riot, till we get
   Its substitute from China, where the tea grows;
But, even here, those paying nature's debt,
       Are wholly negroes."

THE TRIUMPH.

April 10 1871.

Now joy to Barbarossa,
  Upon this April day,
When German landsmen hold the lines
  Of Bowery and Broadway ;4
As erst, a few short weeks ago,
  The pleasant sons of Cork *
Obstructed all thy chosen streets,
  From morn till night, New York!

Through groves of Prussian banners,
  With trumpet, fife and drum,
In pomp of battle's stern array
  And peaceful trade they come;
A Rhine incarnate winding through
  A living double coast,
To where the chiefs of state and town
  Salute the endless host.

---

* St. Patrick's Day celebration.

All glory to the Empire!
    A million plaudits ring,
And glory to the peace that makes
    A Kaiser of a king!
A mighty fortress is our God,
    And we, across the sea,
Join greetings with the Emperor
    To him for victory!

In thunder speaks the cannon
    And swells the glowing song,
While ev'ry high and by-way rolls
    Its multitudes along;
As erst, a few short weeks ago,
    The pleasant sons of Cork
Obstructed all thy chosen streets
    With marshaled throngs, New York.

Now sway the cheering thousands,
    That choke the city's path,
While from a score of throats there comes
    A sudden burst of wrath:

The Triumph.

"Vot for you dries dese bushings here,
  Unt growdings, in der jam?
I dinks you is some Frenchman scared
  Of Unser Fritz, by tam!"

It is a dusty stranger,
  Of aspect most forlorn,
With diff'rent face and speech from them,
  And garments rudely torn,
Who wears a look of frenzied haste,
  And pants, and crowds again;
While ever still they thrust him back—
  These swarming Deutschermen.

"'Tis three o'clock approaches—
  I have a note to meet—
I can't get down to bank or store,
  By any single street—
The cars are all in close blockade,
  And I'm a ruined man
If longer stayed—oh, who will help
  A poor American!"

Thus speaks the frantic stranger,
    They will not let him pass,
Till steps there forward one whose mien
    Proclaims the ruling class:
"Be aisy now, ye Dootchmen there,
    And let the crayture go;
For, sure, it's joost the likes av him
    Once owned the town, ye know.

"The likes av him, be jabers,
    Have gev to us and yez
The right to take the town we're in
    And run it as we plaze;
The likes av him don't vote at all
    When Hans and Pat contind;
But if ye taze the crayture, he
    May bate us in the ind!"

They hear his words of wisdom,
    These sons of fatherland,
And back, to give the stranger way,
    They roll on either hand:

And, like to one of sense bereft,
   Speeds on the wretched man:
Past three o'clock!—a bankrupt is
   The poor American.

Now joy to Barbarossa
   Upon this April day,
When German landsmen hold the lines
   Of Bowery and Broadway;
As erst, a few short weeks ago,
   The pleasant sons of Cork
Obstructed all thy chosen streets,
   From morn till night, New York!

VOX DEI.

"The demons of the mob," said he, "in that masked hell of hate around us,
Were pressing closer on our ranks, with howls and curses to confound us;
Another moment's peace with those who roared for blood, from curb to girder,
Had been the filling of a storm to burst in whirls of fire and murder.

.

"We saw our allies, the police, hemmed in and checked along our borders;
Then faced upon the foe and fired—"
   Yes, soldier, fired without your orders!
Your regiment awaited not the word commanding duly given.
"And yet the order given was, I tell thee, citizen, by heaven!"

Who given by, then, soldier, pray?
    " That question I have solved already ;
'Twas Heaven itself the order gave while yet our
    menaced flanks were steady.
So, let the rescued city say we fired without
    command and blund'red ;
They take from Providence the word who fifty
    slay to save five hundred!"5

THE NINE.

Oft had I heard, in lodgings next to mine,
An eager, manly voice invoke "the Nine!"
And, straightway after, something scraped and boomed,
As though my neighbor strode, and stamped, and fumed.

Sure 'tis a bard, whose burning soul, thought I,
To woo the muses lifts its pleading cry;
And coining verses worthy of his fair,
The lone composer stalks and beats the air.

Once, when we met, I could not help but ask:
'Is ended bravely, sir, your rhyming task?
Our rooms adjoining, I've o'erheard your plea
To all the daughters of Mnemosyne,—

"Heard how you raved—" His staring struck me dumb;
"Mnemosy—who, sir? Oh, see here, now! Come!

The Nine.

I'm swinging Kehoe's clubs, for nerve, before
We meet the base-ball nine from Baltimore.

Brood of high Jove, that haunt Castilian fount!
The classic number, old, by which you count,
And by the poet held divinely fast—
To what Base uses it has come at last!

PRO PATRIA MORI.

The stricken soldier, whitening into death
From reddest flush of strongest life and breath,
Is like the Year, from autumn's fires aglow,
In wintry tempest brought to shroud of snow.
Not his to die where weeping women kneel,
And manhood's specter craves the hand to heal;
From height supreme of manliest might he falls,
'Mid flame and smoke that weave a thousand palls;
One moment meteor of the cloud and blaze,
The next his life-blood ebbs where cattle graze;
Through roars of armies, harrowing the skies,
While fates of nations tremble as they rise,
He hears the captain's call, the gunner's shout,
And in the crash his lion soul goes out.

As follows spring upon the year that died—
Not weak with summer, but in winter's pride—
To write in flow'rs, for epitaph and text,
One season's story that shall rule the next.

Pro Patria Mori.

Come thou with garlands radiant in bloom
To cast upon thine honored soldier's tomb;
With roses, lilies, violets repair,
And in their simple beauty leave them there;
To be, like him, the glory of an hour,
And, in full fragrance, perish by the show'r.
His young, strong life, like theirs, to earth returned,
Makes sweeter store by mother Nature urned,
Undwindling caught, for future years to be
A might and incense deathless for the free.

THE "LAST" MAN.

VENUS herself, at her mirror, beheld not so
    proper a
Beauty as she who looked down from a box at
    the opera,
Scanning with glass all the numerous faces up-
    turned to her,
Heedless that many a heart in the multitude
    burned to her.

Sudden she said to a friend in the chair by the
    side of her—
One of the many who'd thought that ere this
    they'd have died of her—
"Yonder, with head at a sag, and in ulster
    diagonal,
Stands there a man whom I certainly recognize,
    sag an' all!"

Then she grew pensive, nor listened to Gerster's sweet aria:
"Yes, I have known him, although he's grown sleeker and hairier;
Dim recollections, untraceable, seem to reveal to me,
That I have seen yon identical gentleman kneel to me!"

Surely it could not be possible she had the heartlessness
Thus to betray a rejection, with parodied artlessness;
Surely if all her most blinded admirers had been jury,
They'd have decided 'twas adding an insult to injury.

But, from a spell of deep thoughtfulness, verging on tragical,
Changed she to smiles, with a startling celerity magical:—

"Now all the bars of this memory's mystery melt to me!
Bend, and I'll whisper the name of the mortal who's knelt to me."

*　*　*　*　*　*　*　*

So, when you meet her, for fun you may say, if you please, to her,
All that you know of the man who has been on his knees to her;
Making her footsteps obey, as but very few do make her,
He is no other, in fact, than her ladyship's—shoemaker!

EPITHALAMIUM.

THE rose in bloom not surer shows
   That summer's reign is at its prime,
Than that the cheek on which it glows
   Has ripened for the wedding-time.

Ring forth upon the balmy air
   The bells that for the lily swing;
Not they more wonderfully fair
   Than she the bridal courtiers bring.

One moment at the altar bowed,
   With him, her summer prince, beside,
The next, in lace and satin cloud,
   She rises to her throne, a bride.

A something softened in her grace,
   Like twilight from a day in June,
She catches on her mantling face
   The luster of the honeymoon.

And dreams the golden round of days
    That circles thence, like ring from gem,
Shall gleam o'er all her future ways,
    Her life's first summer diadem.

The bridal season's happy hours,
    Its seas divine, its fairy main;—
We pray they die not with the flow'rs,
    Unless, like them, to live again.

BROTHER BLATHERS.

WELL, brother Blathers, on my life, your luck
   In being advertised beats all creation;
Each tempest turns for you into a puff,
   From out your nominal great tribulation.
Walk on your hands around your pulpit's verge,
   Cut pigeon-wings and endless monkey capers,
And what for any other man were shame,
   For you is common fame in all the papers.

I well remember you when hither come,
   A tramping lecturer, from Western college,
How you selected subjects loudly small,
   By noise to hide your want of schoolboy knowledge,
And how the country press, especially,
   Was fond of quoting your Blatheriana
Deceived by platitudes of common gush,
   Roared in conceitedly uncommon manner.

With all your buncombe, though, and postures wild,
  We thought you honest in devout convictions,
And hailed you worthy when you found a church,
  And poured from thence on sin your maledictions.
Not meek and lowly, you exactly seemed ;
  Indeed you had some ways too like a showman ;
Yet when the public crave that sort of thing,
  A little touch of Barnum injures no man.

But when you had that wedding on the stage,
  Some few old-fashioned Christians rather doubted ;
Nor did you gain thereafter their esteem
  Because you higher pranced and louder shouted,
That weekly-paper business, too, of yours,
  Destroyed the faith full many souls had in you ;
Though still they held you not a man of sin,
  So much as one of strange, gymnastic sinew.

The church-debt-raising damaged you the worst,
  In having aspect of a trick unholy;
Nor did your sermons on the city slums
  Remove that sinister impression wholly;
So, at the Presbytery's friendly move,
  To try you on a common fame unflattering,
Your simplest-minded followers could scarce
  Restrain their sympathetic teeth from chattering.

Your weekly-paper publisher could tell
  How you had run his property to tatters,
And then a puff for self had smuggled in,
  Behind his back—with divers other matters.
And your own banker, too, could, say of you:
  "The parson used my name, in cash pedantics
To raise subscriptions to his church's dues—
  Assisters to his cussins's and his antics."

For once the journals' blatant type would prove
  For you no gratifying advertising,
Since, if the charges specified were true,
  About your fall there'd be no more surmising;

But when the trial duly comes at last,
    With all its grand array of proofs alarming—
What is it but your crowning chance to turn
    Just one more flip-flap for the public's charming?

The stern tribunal dwindles, at the start,
    Into a group, as 'twere, of ancient females,
No more in strength and body what 't should be,
    Than smallest beer is like the choicest cream ales;
And as for witnesses to make you wince,
    As early promised, in due form pretentious,
To testify against a man so good,
    They're all, confoundedly, too conscientious.

Thus change the flourishes which made the press
    Above a fancied case of pastoral dolours,
Into a full brass band to your success,
    And you come off, of course, with flying colors.
A fortnight's flaming head-lines, day by day,
    Implying woe for him whom churchmen tackle,
Resolve themselves into a first-class puff
    For that same martyr and his tabernacle.

Brother Blathers.

Hence, Brother Blathers, as I said before,
    Your advertising luck beats all creation,
And so much greater is your gain in print,
    The greater seems your passing tribulation.
Throw somersaults all round your pulpit's verge,
    Stand on your head, cut multifarious capers,
And what for any other man were shame,
    For you is common fame in all the papers.

IN LENT.

So late her lilied beauties caught
    The lustrous radiance of the ball,
Where music's wave of dancers sought
    Her airy footstep's rise and fall,
That even in her sackcloth train
    Some elfin light and motion are,
As eyes turned from it yet retain
    The ray and twinkle of a star.

Upon the twilight veil of Lent
    Her face is like a truant beam,
Escaped from sunlit firmament
    To rest upon a forest stream;
Or, like a daisy of the field,
    That, straying, in a pensive mood,
Is but the lovelier revealed
    Through darkening vistas of the wood.

In Lent.

And here, where brooding shadows soft,
    Through painted windows, touch her head,
And, 'neath the vaulted arches, oft
    Humiliation's prayer is said,
She bows in meekness at a shrine
    That earth's frail vanities should mock,
And blossoms in that shade divine,
    The flower of all the rector's flock.

THE DEAD NAPOLEON.

January 9, 1873.

To the long sleep he lays him down at last,
  Dying an exile in a foreign land;
Lonely of all that thronged his mighty past,
  Save the true wife who clings unto his hand.

Taunts of the foe shall sting his soul no more,
  Dreams of a triumph stir him not to joy;
Only to mourn the glories gone before,
  Left to the weeping mother of his boy.

Let the coarse lip be curled in fierce disdain,
  Now that an empire lives not in his glance;
Let the rude jeer be pointed once again
  At the departed majesty of France!

Borne to his grave, he will not feel it now;
  Lying in sepulcher, he cannot hear;
And the imperial bending of his brow
  Smoothes into death beneath a woman's tear.

The Dead Napoleon.

Mock at the head in dust that lieth down,
    Once for its wearing what the mobsman scorns;
Echo the rabble's hatred of a crown,
    E'en as it spurned and hated one of thorns!

To the lone dead it bringeth naught of shame,
    That on his fortune set a wintry sun ;
Something sublime of his great kinsman's name
    Dwells with the cold and still Napoleon.

In the bleak land where once that kinsman's star
    Paled at a burning city's stoic scoff,
His was the hand relighting, brighter far,
    Torched by the guns that rent the Malakhoff.

By the same sword that brought him from the throne,
    Breaking in battle mightier than he,
Freedom's Italia gave he to her own,
    From the white Alpine summits to the sea.

Through the dread woe and shadow of Sedan,
    Crownless the empire catches as it flits,
Fire from a Solferino and the man
    True to her memories of Austerlitz.

Queen of the dead, beside her dead she bows
    In her own passion France the yet accurst;
Helpless of him, the last her pride to rouse,
    Borne to his tomb in distant Chiselhurst.

But, by the matchless glories of the past,
    Marvel of story for the tongue and pen,
Cæsar shall come unto his own at last,
    When her avenging eagles soar again!

HUMOR'S ILIAD.

THE liquid laugh hilarious hails the jest
   From trifling tongue, or facile fancy's store,
And wit's unwisest zanyable zest
   Awakes the long-resounding, ribald roar.

But scarce a smile on lip the lightest greets
   The masking mirth of many a mournful thing,
That, grimly grave, has unctuous under-beats,
   As 'neath the turgid tide's the bubbling spring.

Full often souls in silvery song supreme,
   By bodies bent to groaning grief are borne;
Full oft the depths of dreariest drivel teem
   With marks of Momus, merry as the morn.

The simple sophist's garrulous "Go West!"—
   The native newsman's fearful foreign flights—
The doleful doctrine Darwin has exprest—
   The sermon Spurgeon seriously writes—

All are but jokes on yawning Yankee youth—
    A humor spun at transatlantic speed—
The slyest slap at scientific truth—
    A comic treatment of the churchman's creed.

In them an awkward aiming to amuse,
    Through gloomy gravity, imperfect gleams;
Bewilders brain 'twixt grin and groan to choose,
    And half of humor, half of horror seems.

More mortals mean to find facetious fame
    Than can command the cachinnating sound;
Their words and works, despite themselves, are tame,
    And, failing to be funny, prove profound.

Lo, Huxley harping Protoplastic pleas,
    And Stuart Mill to woman-warring won;
They turned, perchance, to tangled themes like these,
    From palled perplexity to plan a pun.

Full many a man of quaintly-comic whim,
    Has sadly sighed when critics crude have spoke,
Because, for sober savant taking him,
    His metaphysics made them miss his joke.

The boldest book bewildering the breast,
  The strangest words by skeptic science said,
May shrine untold, unutterable jest,
  Through impulse impotent to make it read.

No longer lag a limit to install
  Between the gay and grave, in petty poise;
But learn—save heaven's high writ—to laugh at all
  Of knowledge, nonsense, knavery and noise.

THE JESTER'S BURIAL.

In the land of Aibmuloc,
   Lo, a host, in motley drest,
Bear, in last, fantastic march,
   Mij, the jester, to his rest!

Hues of crimson, blue and gold,
   Quaint and garish, glow and shine;
E'en the shrouded cap and bells
   Nod and tinkle down the line.

These, the colors of his life,
   Round the sable of his bier,
Mock the pity of the sight,
   Like a rainbow on a tear.

Through the roll of muffled drums,
   Through the trumpet's measured blare,
Steal the distant medley sounds
   Of a ribald, dancing air!

The Jester's Burial.

His in life to follow them,
   When the dizzy whirl was fast,
Blending ghastly with a knell,
   Now they follow him at last.

In the tinsel home he left
   May be those whose eyes are dim;
But in all the gazing crowd
   None there are to weep for him.

Looking where his corse is borne,
   They, who bore his laughing rule,
Smile at later folly's birth,
   In the dying of the fool.

Not a sigh to honor now
   All the merry jests he gave;
Not a friendly hand to cast
   Flow'rs upon the jester's grave.

One is dead whose daring mirth
   Pride abashed and honor vext,
Virtue mocked and truth defied—
   One is dead—and live the next!

Winds the dismal pageant show
   In its tawdry pomp along,
Like the burden of a dirge
   Striving with a drinker's song.

What shall be the preacher's words
   When before the cross he brings
Pleadings for the motley fool
   To the mighty King of kings?

In the land of Aibmuloc
   They have cited to the crown,
Not the wisdom of the wise,
   But the colors of the clown;—

From the glories of the court,
   From the barony of gold,
Spurned the slower modest worth,
   For the folly that is bold.

Poor the prize that merit wins,
   Toiling in a grave behest,
When the treasures of a realm,
   Are the guerdon of a jest!

God is just; and who shall say,
  If, where none may dare to mock,
Mij, the jester, he will blame,
  Or the land of Aibmuloc?

BALLADS AND BROADSIDES.

A FABLE OF FINANCE.

THERE was a rich banker in Wall street renowned,
With clerks a small army and desks all around;
His offices stately presented a mass
Of fancy black walnut and costly plate-glass.

CHORUS.

Properly rebuking impertinent curiosity as to a matter of strictly private concern:

In the banking, insurance or railroading line,
'Tis the custom your rivals in style to outshine;
But if pressed with the question, whence cometh the pay?
I must answer—Ri-tooral, ri-tooral, li-day.

This banker received the deposits of those
Who wanted them safe from burglarious foes;
And likewise of people with funds to invest
In ventures returning the interest best.

Chorus.

Explaining how you pay your interest upon the deposits left with you, and yet make a small stake by the generous transaction:

When you give me your riches to keep till you call,
In a stock or a loan do I put them out all.
But supposing stock falls, or the loan's lost, you say?
Then it's—Tooral, ri-tooral, ri-tooral, li-day!

No end of accounts in this manner came in,
Of anxious to save, and of anxious to win;
And ev'ry one said, what a fortune must be
Inclosed in the vaults of this man's treas-u-ry.

Chorus.

Showing that therein exists a trifling error, scarcely worth mentioning:

It's quite banking custom such fortunes to lend
To a railroad or bank for its next dividend;
Then if all goes on well there's usurious pay,
If it doesn't—Ri-tooral, ri-tooral, li-day!

A Fable of Finance.

At last the rich banker in finances skilled,
With schemes for a highway most novel was filled;
The same to be called, when its tracks were all laid,
The Huge-Universal-Mid-Bound'ry-Up-Grade.

CHORUS.

Coolly setting forth the geography of this great undertaking, and its sources of rich revenues.

'Twas from pole unto pole that this highway should go,
To the great open sea of the Arctic, you know;
Many tourists take up, bears and seals bring away,
With a—Tooral, ri-tooral, ri-tooral, li-day!

He called on the rich to subscribe for the shares,
And also the poor who would be millionaires.
'Twas interest in gold they would pay in a trice
Secured by a good bond and mortgage on ice.

Chorus.

Defining the great ease of manner with which aforesaid interest could be paid:

From the money paid down for the stock, he could meet
All the interest prescribed, till the road was complete;
And, at last, if the work didn't happen to pay,
Why the shares were—Ri-tooral, ri-tooral, li-day!

With praise of the scheme ev'ry paper was full,
And each money-editor in it a "bull;"
'Twill greatly develop our country, they said,
And show if John Franklin's alive or is dead.

Chorus.

Delicately intimating why journalism is never backward in encouraging a noted public enterprise of this nature:

There are journals so sanguine of railroad success,
That a part of the stock they themselves may possess;

And if how they came by it you'd have them betray,
They will tell you—Ri-tooral, ri-tooral, li-day!

The banker's depositors caught at the thing,
And cried, let us into this gold-bearing ring:
And so did the people all over the land,
Who other stocks had, or the money on hand.

Chorus.

Expressive of the childlike trust reposed in the wisdom and honor of the few by the many:

If a few wealthy men of good mercantile fames,
To an enterprise lend their respectable names,
It must surely be just what its managers say—
Or the signers are—Tooral, ri-tooral, li-day!

Then ten savings banks purchased shares in it too,
And banks of all kinds bought the stock as it grew;
And model trust companies took it in trade,—
This Huge-Universal-Mid-Bound'ry-Up-Grade.

CHORUS.

Indicating the judicious policy followed by such institutions in such case:

If your trust-institution, your bank, or its like,
On a good speculation believes it can strike,
It is not slow to reap what it can in that way;
Though it sometimes—Ri-tooral, ri-tooral, li-day!

At last there were millions invested therein,
And waiting for trips on the road to begin,
When some one discovered, and told with a bawl,
No road of the kind had been builded at all!

CHORUS.

Informing the reader how it might have happened that the H. U. M. B. U. G. was not built:

In the cost of proclaiming the bonds are for sale
And of working the market that holders shan't fail,
Such a very large sum is exhausted, some way,
That the railroad itself is—Ri-tooral, li-day!

Down tumbled the stock, with a rush, at the sound,
And banks, brokers, buyers, in frenzy were found;
And when to the banker the multitude went,
They found he'd "suspended" and paid not a cent!

CHORUS.

To be sung with great animation in the nearest bankrupt court:

There are railroads too many this day in the land,
And the stock of the best scarcely profits the hand;
But to buy into more, with the hope that they'll pay,
Is a—Tooral, ri-tooral, ri-tooral, li-day!

CONDENSED TRAGEDIES.

Vide the daily papers.

Greene saw the boat was off, and wildly flew for it.
The life insurance folks cried, "Let 'em sue for it."

Jane used camphene to light her fire the faster.
"We lay her to her rest," intoned the pastor.

Smith blew the gas out ere the bed he glided for,
Leaving his family quite unprovided for.

To learn if charged, Jones breathed into his fowling-piece.
His widow's uncle will support his howling niece.

Brown thought he'd flirt with Simpson's wife a little.
The jury stood a dozen for acquittal.

Condensed Tragedies.

"I'll shave," said Ruth, of woman's rights the forerunner.
"The razor must have slipped," observed the coroner.

Stiles jumped to reach a moving rail-car's platform.
A home's bereavement shocking is in that form.

"What whisky one can stand," said Tompkins, "try, oh, let's."
His sleep is sweet beneath the early violets.

His shop-girls put on top-most floor did Blaney.
After the fire they didn't count so many.

Jinks tried to stop, by hand, a something-or-other-in' saw.
"My daughter's next shan't smoke," remarked his mother-in-law.

THE COMMON LOT.

It was a solid Boston man,
    Majestic as a stork,
Who thought to have another scan—
    A skeptic from New York—
Without preparing for the thing,
    His city's ancient pride,
That Common which she thinks a king
    Would joy to be inside.

He took thereto, by devious ways,
    The infidel in charge,
Through winding streets in grievous maze,
    And alleys small and large;
Not saying whither he would lead,
    Nor yet intending to,
Until the transcendental mead
    Should burst upon their view.

At last a sudden corner turned,
    There beamed upon the sight
That vision the Bostonian yearned
    To have his friend delight;
And then—alas! the bitter cup
    Commended on the spot!—
"Why don't you build your city up?
Who owns that vacant lot?"

THE COMIC CHRISTIAN CLERGYMAN.

Of all the incongruities terrestrial nature shows—
The splendid peacock's horrid voice, the thorn beneath the rose,
The lowest range of reason joined to beauty's highest air—
There's none, for shocking mortal sense of fitness, can compare
    With the comic Christian clergyman,
    One of the latest time.

By bonds of poor estate in youth to humblest schools confined,
And then, mayhap, in knowledge versed—of Western college kind;
Too crude to doctor bodies sick, or as attorney plod,
He's bold to dose the dying soul, and prate the laws of God—
    Is the comic Christian clergyman,
    One of the latest time.

Within the rustic meeting house installed at first, he sees
That something of a startling sort with common taste agrees,
And burns therein to emulate your city preacher's fame,
By saying things unorthodox, and earning thus the name
    Of a comic Christian clergyman,
    One of the latest time.

'Tis whispered in the mighty town, a "stunner" new is found!
(Perhaps a funny lecture there he tries, the way to sound,)
Then comes a picked committee forth, of churchmen great and small,
To hear, to laugh with aching sides, and straightway give a call,
    To this comic Christian clergyman,
    One of the latest time.

They build a spacious church for him, fantastic in
 its style,
With graces of the play-house form in gallery
 and aisle;
And on a structure like a stage the arch-per-
 former stands,
Prepared to beat the best, if need, by walking on
 his hands,
 Like a comic Christian clergyman,
 One of the latest time.

Then to the sacred edifice the population pour,
With expectation of a treat surpassing all before;
The sermon is to show that Paul was fogyish,
 because
He hadn't been a Congressman—and this evokes
 applause
 For the comic Christian clergyman,
 One of the latest time.

He coughs, and then goes on to say, that Paul,
 in all his life,
Appeared opposed to woman's rights—but never
 had a wife;

For had he owned the sex's sway, not thus speak
out he'd dare!
And all his hearers laugh and say—he surely had
him there!
    Did our comic Christian clergyman,
    One of the latest time.

The clap of hands, the trill of mirth, respond to
him throughout
His most facetious ministry and wild rhetoric
rout;
And when his windy book appears, uncouth of
tone and wit,
A more amusing moral work, they say, was
never writ
    By a comic Christian clergyman,
    One of the latest time.

His greatest joke of all, howe'er, is when his
church is burned,
And he and all his motley flock upon the town
are turned:

"Since Providence makes light of it, our church
   was naught!" He! He!
"Let's hire a theater, and hold a fancy-fair
   levee,"
      Says the comic Christian clergyman,
      One of the latest time.

This giving of a hum'rous twist to serious mishap,
Another gorgeous feather adds unto the jester's cap;
But when he marries, on the stage, in masquerade, a pair
He's advertised to come and be a feature of the fair—
      What a comic Christian clergyman,
      One of the latest time!

Not ours to doubt his honesty, since mean the right he may;
Yet in another manner, far, the Master walked his way;

The high of soul, the meek of heart, the humble
 unto death,
How different, in his solemn truth, was he of
 Nazareth
  From the comic Christian preacher,
  One of the latest time.

When gather dark the clouds upon the spirit in
 despair,
And thunders of the judgment roll around it
 ev'rywhere,
For him that gave the scoffer's sneer the potency
 to kill,
What if the dying hand should point—and e'en
 be pointing still—
  At a comic Christian clergyman,
  One of the latest time!

BALLOON BALLADS.

As inflated by different illustrious types of poetic genius.

BALLOON HIM OF THE REPUBLIC.

BY J—LIA W—RD H—WE.

You may call it "she," the aerostat that breasts the balmy blue,
You may speak of "her" ascending till the earth is lost to view;
But the sex contemned as feminine has naught with it to do,
  Nor assists its soaring on.

In the buoyancy of gases it may hover wide and far,
With a row of bearded faces in its viriclusive car;
From its company of voyagers excluded women are,
  As the thing goes soaring on.

On the earth a jealous tyrant, so in airy currents
    high,
It is man that layeth woman like a useless bauble
    by;
Scarcely worth his worldly notice, shall he take
    her to the sky,
        When himself goes soaring on?

Then assign a proper gender to your bubble of
    the breeze,
Let it be a virile he, or it, or anything you please,
For 'tis not a she, by any means, that sails side-
    real seas,
        And for man goes soaring on.

MOSE.

BY BR—T H—RTE.

Duffer's Bar, 1872.

—Here! another round jerk us,
    And trust me for paying—
  So, as I was saying,
We went up from the circus;

Only us two,
Me and my crew,
A goggle-eyesing, pig-despising,
Curly-headed Jew.

Why, ballooning's no trouble;
When cut is your lashing,
If nothing gets smashing,
You go up like a bubble—
Only, you see,
'Twixt you and me,
An extra poun' may bring you down a
Little bit too free.

And we had it that day, too!
Ahead was the water,
In which we'd be caught, or
Must rise higher, and lay to.
Still we sank on,
Ballast all gone;
Without a hope to loop a rope to
Aught the land upon.

"Well, let one of us perish
  For sake of the other—
  You've been like a brother—
For my life I'm don't-care-ish,"
    Whispered so true,
    Moses, my crew;
"I'm bound to jump it, like or lump it,
    Overboard for you!"

I'd give five hundred dollars.
  But just to put eye on
  (Excuse me for cryin')
The dear chap that I allers
    Mourn for since then—
    Seen not again—
As a dear departed, noble-hearted
    Miracle of men.

What is that you are saying?
  "Suppose he ain't dead, hey?
  But struck on his head, hey?"
With my feelings you're playing,—

Do I see true?
Why—*Mose*—it's YOU!—
You goggle-eyesing, pig-despising,
Curly-headed Jew!

LAUS THETIS.

BY ALG—RN—N CH—RLES SW—NB—RNE.

As on Sepia's shoreland the golden,
   Where the waters of Thessaly shine,
Sprang Peleus, in the days that were olden,
   After azure-tressed Thetis divine;
As he strove in her flying to reach her,
   Whom by Zeus to his reaching was given;
As he followed the swift-footed creature
       Of heaven;

As he urged but his going the faster,
   When the nymph to a serpent transformed;
As his will was unswerving her master,
   When as fire or as torrent she stormed;

As he mocked at her lioness-roaring,
  And still knew the beloved of Poseidon ;
As his hell changed, by Cheiron's imploring,
    To Eden ;

So the vessel that soars to the azure
  A cerulean Thetis pursues,
Through the serpentine cloudy embrasure,
  With its chryselephantinous hues.
Though the lightning and tempest, like devils,
  Should oppose,by their fury unriven,
The balloon beats at last the blue levels
    Of heaven !

INFATUOSITY.

BY TH—S C—R—YLE.

At the tale of a flatulent sphere,
  In a flimsy contrivance of strings,
They suppose to the planets they're near,
  On their gas-house-bituminous wings.

Never knowing which way they may go,
   Nor the moment in which they may drop;
To their asinine brothers below
   They're as ants on the peg of a top.

It's as well that the race should be free
   From the idiots wasting its sup:
And, since some won't go down, as we see,
   'Tis a blessing that some can go up.

'Twixt the zanies of fame and of pelf
   I've become so disgusted of late,
That I'd fain have the world to myself,
   With my Goethe and Frederick the Great.

THE SAINTED DAMOSEL.

BY D—NTE G—BRIEL R—S—TTI.

It was a sainted damosel
From heavenly casement leaned and prayed;
   "The sun and stars below are well,
   And shines th' ethereal asphodel,
And hovering angels chorus swell;
   But I'm a lonely maid!"

Balloon Ballads.

The winds, enamored, heard the pray'r,
That made her snowy bosom throb ;
  And, waving wild their arms of air,
  As she her own so soft and fair,
Gave echoing answer of despair,
    In zeph'rous, soughing sob.

A mortal, wandering round the moon,
The dreary moaning overheard,
  And being in a large balloon,
  Much ballast he cast over soon,
Till, fluttering like a dove in June,
    He rose to heavens third.

" Why murmur, lovely saint ? " he cried,
" In realms of radiant, endless bliss ? "
  " Because I yearn for thee," she sighed ;
  " Oh, pause, young man, and here abide.
I'm sorrowing for the world denied,
    And lonely am in this."

"I cannot stay, alas!" he ple'd,
"The world you name, still claims my aid.
Are no young men in heaven instead?"
"Ah, yes; but they're *so* good!" she said;
And piteous sighed, as on he sped,
"Oh, I'm a lonely maid!"

UNDERWRITEOUSNESS.

HE rose with early day
And sought the broad highway,
His features fine effulgent with the good he meant to do;
By three score-years-and-ten
An elder amongst men,
This morning made his manful youth return as good as new.

With one benignant roar
He tripped from door to door,
His sparkling spectacles agleam with pity's purest light:
"Turn out; and give your best
To succor the distrest!"
And thundered at each threshold's verge with rude, resounding might.

Up went the windows high,
Between the earth and sky,
While heads in rumpled rows came forth to answer the alarm;
And all were much surprised
When they had recognized
The good, gray-headed gentleman who'd broken slumber's charm.

His form impatient swelled,
As louder yet he yelled—
"Lose not a minute more, my friends, but haste and give your aid;
A mighty city* swept
By fire while you have slept,
Craves quick compassion to repair the ruthless ruin made!

"One hundred thousand souls,
Where flame in torrent rolls,
Burned out of house and home and hope, must helped this moment be;

---
* Chicago, October, 1871.

And bankrupt at the call
Are underwriters all—
Except the Non-Combustion Fire Insurance Company!

"Turn out with might and main,
I beg of you again;
Nor lose a moment in the strife of sending succor straight;
For money, food and dress,
In want and nakedness,
Woe-wasted men all weary watch, and weeping women wait!"

They paused to hear no more,
But flew to give their store—
The rich the richer rivaling, the poor to proffer pence;
And surging to the street,
With money, clothes and meat,
Inquired the rightful railway routes to haste the harvest hence.

The minds of high and low,
Compassionate aglow,
Thought only if the giver's gift would first of
    freight afford;
    While ever, here and there,
    With urging voice and air,
Besought that bustling gentleman large lending
    to the Lord.

"You railroad men," he cried,
"Expressmen, too, beside,
And drivers divers, different, of costly coach, or
    cart,
    If you are Christian men,
    Give free conveyance, then,
To bounty boundlessly bestowed by human hand
    and heart.

"Heap high the great and small
Free off'rings from us all;
For smallest succor sent with speed will warmest
    welcomed be.

Underwriteousness.

    The underwriters best
    Are beggared with the rest—
Except the Non-Combustion Fire Insurance
    Company!"

•

    The people thus inspired,
    To nobler giving fired,
On cart and carriage, truck and train, their precious parcels piled;
    While wondering as they ran,
    What blessed kind of man
Was this who claimed complete control and went with waiting wild?

    And yet he spurred them on,
    When train on train had gone,
And called for contributions casting Crœsus in the shade;
    " But fifty thousand, you!
    Who're richer than a Jew?
Why, where's the wealth your wit has won in tributary trade?

"A hundred thousand make
Your charitable stake,
Or find the furtive fiend of fire some day your
    debtor dread!
And you, who offer four
Of thousands full a score—
I'm 'shamed to shake the halting hand that heeds
    such haggling head!

"More money, yet, I say:
Or there will come a day,
When, should our sov'reign city, here, its own
    consuming see,
Ourselves may lose our all—
Except the risks that fall
Upon the Non-Combustion Fire Insurance Company!"

Then all the people cheered,
As though there had appeared
A saint supreme amongst them, driving each to
    duty due;

Underwriteousness.

  And followed him in ranks,
  From humblest shops to banks,
To do the good that underwriters damaged didn't do.

  But when the day was o'er,
  And ceased the rush and roar,
So charged with Christian charity and prodigal of pelf,
  The question did arise,
  'Mid more or less surprise,
Who is this good old gentleman, and what gave he himself?

  It proved, in the event,
  That he was president
Of that same Non-Combustion Fire Insurance he did laud:
  And as for what he gave,
  The uninsured to save—
He hadn't given anything, the venerable fraud!

THE BOSTON MAN.

November, 9, 1872.

SLOWLY a Boston man
    Fried in his store,
Where, seeking salvage, he'd
    Gained upper floor;
Singing, " A threnody
    Write for me now,
Julia Ward—Julia Ward—
    Julia Ward Howe!"

Came a fire company
    Under the sash,
Rearing the ladders there,
    Quick as a flash:
Crying, 'To rescue thee
    Norwich ascends;
Boston man, Boston man,
    Help bring thy friends!"

Peered then the Boston man
  Down through the smoke,
O'er where the ladder-end
  Casement had broke;
Asking with dignity—
  "Answer me true—
Norwich men, Norwich men,
  What would ye do?"

Up spake a Norwich man,
  Poised on a rung,
Breaking the sashes in,
  Red sparks among—
"We, by thy city's light,
  Come to assist;
Boston man, Boston man,
  Give us thy fist!"

Back sprang the Boston man,
  Splendidly proud,
Saying, while flames around
  Wove him a shroud:

"Outside assistance is
  Of him the scorn,
Gentlemen, gentlemen,
  Who's Boston-born!!"6

●

Wildly the Norwich men
  Swarmed up, amain,
Vainly to rescue him
  Seen not again;
And e'en a threnody
  Writes for him now
Julia Ward—Julia Ward—
  Julia Ward Howe!

CHICKEN AND EGGS ARE OUT.

A FARM BALLAD OF THE PERIOD.

Go, hide the coop, there, Betsey, and nail the hen-house stout;
We've city boarders comin', and chicken and eggs are out.
Since Will M. Carleton made us the talk so far and wide,
There's been no end of town-folks for summer board applied.7

The first one writin' to us,—that preacher, as he said,—
About our little rampage and making-up had read;
Our story 'd touched his feelin's, and would we strive to take
His fam'ly for the season, and some deduction make?

He only wanted quiet, and simply sun and air,
With eggs and milk and chickens, and such-like country fare;
He wouldn't press for oysters; but veg'tables and fruit,
Could not be served too frequent, himself and wife to suit.

For this he'd give three dollars, for each, all round, per week,
And hoped our house was roomy—why, dang his 'tarnal cheek!
If I was worth a million, and twice as much he paid,
I wouldn't feed a stomach by preachin' empty made.

The next one seekin' quarters was sick, he wrote, of style,
And wished his dame and daughters to rusticate a while;
For, what with Saratoga, and Newport, in the past,
He'd found his purse and patience were runnin' out too fast.

And, would we b'lieve, our story had moved them all to tears;
And had we first-floor bed-rooms, with bath-rooms in their rears?
They wouldn't ask for livin' in costly city way;
But milk and eggs and poultry, must have three times a day.

The three young girls' dyspepsia would call for graham bread,
And Madame took her coffee at early dawn in bed;
And for himself at breakfast, he'd take a beef-steak rare,
Nor think ten dollars, weekly, for all, much more than fair.

It's one thing for a poet our honest hearts to praise,
And another, keepin' boarders, that profit us no ways;
I answered, quite sarcastic, "Just call when you're about,
And find, by knockin' vainly, that **Betsey** and I are out!"

Then there was what-you-call-him, the scrawling writer chap,
Who'd read the poem careful about our old mishap,
And thought a woman wrote it, because she made the claim,
And said that if she didn't, to cross her was a shame.

"We can't go back on women," his self-same letter ran,
At least 'twould be unworthy a literary man;
Our mother's sex we worship, or we should be but churls;
I hope you've got for neighbors some lively country girls.

"My wife is at her mother's, and I am out at grass;
With a taste for new-churned butter, and cream, and rural lass.
Just give me trout for breakfast, and then what else you please,
And a little apple-brandy to wash down bread and cheese.

" I only ask for freedom to come and go at will,
And the right of fishin' Sundays by the nearest water-mill ;
And a dash of sage and onions with the canvas-duck at noon,
And the use of team and wagon whenever there's a moon.

" We authors don't reap fortunes, and so you'll make your charge
Proportioned to my calling, and anything but large ;
I'll pay you, on my honor, you needn't fear a bit—
As soon as my book can compass a publisher for it."

If I'd a gift of scribblin', so glib as that and cool,
I'd make a mountain of dollars by teachin' a writin' school.
" If ever your brass," I wrote him, " some folks should take for tin,
Be certain, for ref'rence, always, that Betsey and I are in ! "

No end of other letters I've had to answer, too,
From people all over natur', with dollars a mighty few,
And over the hill to the poor house we might as well repair,
As deal with the city boarders who want but country fare.

We've got one fam'ly comin', from southward, I suppose,
Who never have heard about us in verse, nor yet in prose.
They merely want, they told us, a breath of the new-mown hay,
And the kind of dinner-table that we'd set anyway.

Between the town-folks selfish, who think a farm is made
Of eggs and chickens and dairy, for which no cash is paid,
And them, more free and foolish, who never think a mite,
But come, when they'd do better, at home, a precious sight—

We, farming kind, get riley, to find the breed so flat;
And where's our human natur' if we made naught by that?
We give to the ones we welcome potatoes, pork and greens,
With apple pie and doughnuts, and a spice of corn and beans.

But as for milk and poultry, and things in skin and shell,
We send them down to the city, for they were made to sell;
And if 'twas them they wanted, these folks who range and roam,
They ought to know where to buy them, and that is in town, at home.

So hide the coop, there, Betsey, and nail the hen-house stout;
We've city boarders comin', and chicken and eggs are out;

And, what is still more pesky, to happen the self-
 same day,
Our milk is all out, likewise—until they have
 gone away!

THE TRUCKEE REGATTA.

This Students' Regatta is all very well
For your Latin and Greek university swell;
And callow collegians of Newspaper Row
May be ready to stand on their heads at the show.

But people in general vote it a bore,
If they haven't a brother, or son at the oar;
While I, who have seen what a boatman can do,
Do not care to take stock in a Sophomore crew.

For what I call rowing, from shoulder to knee,
There were none like the men of the roaring Truckee,
Who made up a match in the year 'Fifty-nine,
In the camp of the old Santa Barbara mine.

The long rainy season at last had set in,
With its floods from the hills, that came down with a din;

They settled the race at the Crystal saloon,
In the time between deals of the game Vingt-et-un.

'Twixt Mexican Dick and his partner in trade,
And a Yank and his partners, the challenge was made,
In dug-outs to paddle up stream in the rain,
That a purse of ten ounces the winners might gain.

The Yank and his men had been whalers down East;
For they came from New Bedford, or said so, at least;
And Mexican Dick and his party made boast
They had served in a frigate along by the coast.

No training or "coach" for such oarsmen as these,
But a license to eat and to drink at their ease;
They'd muscles like giants, to lift or to pull,
And were tough in a wrestle when empty or full.

The day of the race was a sight to behold,
And the river was snowy with foam as it rolled;

Yet down in their dugouts the gold-diggers sat,
And were off like the wind, at the wave of a hat.

You talk about rowing! I shall not show how
They were manned for their work at the stroke and the bow;
Nor pause to describe a particular burst,
As, with struggle tremendous, each strove to be first.

You need not be bothered to hear how they bent,
And their ponderous boats through the element sent,
Or how, for an instant, they'd stand in the air,
In a manner like spiders, or trestle-work, there.

The story is ended when one thing is read:
Though the dugout of Yank made the finish ahead—
"Not traversed the course," all the judges did say;
"She was out of the water two-thirds of the way!"

BILLIARDS.

BY A RETIRED AMATEUR.

In the days when I Spotted the Ball,
   Where my meeting Miss Cue none should mock at,
Many Runs did I make at the call
   Of her sire, who was great on the Pocket.

Nothing less than a Count of three-score,
   If he'd had his own way, he'd have chosen;
And her cheek grew so chalk-like, I swore
   That the Red and the White, there, were frozen.

All in vain had I Banked for the lead
   With a parent whose Draw beat me hollow;
Yet he made not a Point in his greed,
   That I didn't surpass with a Follow.

Till, at last, an unfortunate Break,
  For the fortune he'd lost made him mourner;
When a spout at three balls did I take
  To deliver him out of his corner.

Then he gratefully gave me a Miss—
  Never barring a Push that was tinglish—
And he said: "You may win by a Kiss;
  But, be sure, don't put on too much English."

Those were days when a shot off the Spot
  Was the end of all foul-playing wrangle;
And a Miss, made for safety or not,
  Came with only a good honest Angle.

They were times of more Phelan than these,
  When to Nurse on the Rail had been brassy;
And the French of a stroke that could please
  Wasn't what it is now—"Lor! a *masse!*"

A STOOP TO CONQUER.

My Reversible Stoop and Front-door Bell Dissuader
  Is what I'd commend unto housekeepers all;
Of your lives' daily pests the unfailing evader,
  And matchless for keeping them out of the hall.
The top platform of stone, or of wood, has a pivot
  On either side, hid in adjustable sheath,
And who clutches your street-bell, a ringing to give it,
  It quickly transfers to a chamber beneath.

'Tis a beauty of this most benignant invention,
  That they who stand on it in manner polite,
Would not ever find out its ingenious intention,
  'Till told, from door opened, to step in aright.
Your connections and friends and respectable callers
  Don't tramp to your threshold as though 'twere their own,

As do those whom my stoop is designed to make
  fallers,
  Because sure to tread the whole width of the
    stone.

Here's the beggar that comes ev'ry day, spite of
  warning—
  That all you can give is for others than her;
She goes scuffling her brogans up each step this
  morning,
  And drops out of sight with a magical whir!
Then there follows a man with a patent clothes-
  wringer,
  Whose nails scratch the bell-pull as downward
    he shoots;
And a prater of Wheeler and Wilson, or Singer,
  Who sinks as he scrapes on your door-sill his
    boots.

Then a beggar once more; and a youth who's
  inquiring
  If this is a number he sees that it's not;
And a female book-agent, close converse desir-
  ing :—
  Each vanishes swift from the view like a shot.

Comes a wand'rer reduced, with a wedding-ring solid,
  His precious late wife's, 'tis his anguish to sell;
With some tickets for church-fair a juvenile stolid;
  A beggar again;—down they flutter, pell-mell.

Next, the person who asks: Where is Mr. Jinks living?
  Quick followed by one with tape, needles to show;
And a book-agent, bland, to rebuffs all forgiving;
  A beggar; and man wild to shovel off snow.
One who'd ask but the gift of an old pair of trousers;
  And one who'd inquire if you've tin-ware to mend;
A purveyor of pie-apples, called by him "rousers"—
  One after another they quickly descend.

Then an old individual sucking his finger,
  To ask for the doctor, who's two doors beyond;

A Stoop to Conquer.

And a tramp of the class that will stamp while
    they linger
  Till you with a spoon for their coffee respond ;
A demoralized foreigner raising subscription
  To take him back home for his dear one's
    delight;
And your hand-organ girl, who requires no description ;
  A beggar or two—and they go out of sight.

At your own certain hours, when 'tis filled to full
    measure,
  Examine the cage of detention you may,
Picking out of the contents what suits your good
    pleasure,
  And throwing the worthless remainder away.
Once a housekeeper looked on my stoop with
    such rapture,
  She left it all day to its saving of breath,
And then found that the book-agents, four, of her
    capture,
  Had talked all the others completely to death.

Were it not that occasional friends from the
    country
  Go down, from promiscuous scrapes of their
    feet,
I'm not certain but, really, that I'd to be blunt,
    try,
  The book-agent system the job to complete.
As it is, that past slave to the ring, servant-maid,
    or,
  Whoever has 'tended your portal, will find
My Reversible Stoop and Front-door Bell Dis-
    suader
  A blessing, indeed, and a boon to mankind.

THE POLISHED LEGAL GENTLEMAN.

Your Chesterfields and Grandisons were, very
   probably,
Examples to our ancestors of true gentility;
But how to do the courteous thing in courtliest
   final way,
Was left to be exemplified in this, our later day,
   By a polished legal gentleman,
   One of the present time.

We'll say a case has come to him, quite difficult,
   no doubt,
Commanding all his skill profound to make its
   justice out;
Proportioned to retaining fee, he sees at once its
   strength—
Or vows that what it lacks therein shall be made
   up in length,—
   Like a polished legal gentleman,
   One of the present time.

If witnesses upon the side his talents represent
Are of a class repugnant to all decent sentiment,
Or if in number they are weak, and, maybe, circumspect,
He'll foil their cross-examining by howling " I object ! "
  Like a polished legal gentleman,
   One of the present time.

Upon the other side, perchance, is evidence complete,
All technical perversion of the statutes to defeat ;
And they are unimpeachable who come to testify ;
He knows a trick to beat them yet—" without an alibi "—
  Like a polished legal gentleman,
   One of the present time.

Old Mr. Knickerbocker's form is seen upon the stand,
Whose whole career shines spotless in the annals of the land ;

He tells what makes the plaintiff's cause look
 ominously dim—
(Just wait till comes our counsel's turn to cross-
 examine him,
  Like a polished legal gentleman,
   One of the present time.)

"Your name is 'Knickerbocker?' Ah!—'from
 trade retired'—I see!
Have you been ever sent unto the Pen-i-ten-
 tiary?
No blust'ring now! * * * 'Object,' indeed! I'll
 to the court defer,
That it is competent to show his previous char-
 ac-ter,"
  Roars a polished legal gentleman,
   One of the present time.

"I'll thrash you, sir!—I'll—I'll not stay to be insulted so!"
The venerable witness cries, indignantly aglow.
7

"What's that? You cannot bulldoze ME, my man,
    as you will find!"
Replies the brave possessor of the true judicial
    mind,
    Like a polished legal gentleman,
    One of the present time.

The court here interposes, to allay unseemly
    strife,
"A question more outrageous I ne'er heard in all
    my life!"
The blandest of all voices says: "Your honor. I
    submit;
That admonition leaves no choice, for me, but
    heeding it"—
    Like a polished legal gentleman,
    One of the present time.

"Now, Mr. Knickerbocker, pray, your temper
    hot restrain,
And we'll get on as pleasantly as good old friends
    again.

The Polished Legal Gentleman.

You have a daughter, I believe, who's married,
  as they say?"
(The question he insinuates in quite a genial
  way,
  Like a polished legal gentleman,
  One of the present time.)

"Well, sir, I have; and what of that?" the witness sharp replies.
"Why, then, my man" (ferociously), "just drop all useless lies,
And answer, ON YOUR OATH, if she, ere to said marriage forced,
Had not, by former husband, been somewhere out west, divorced?"
  Yells a polished legal gentleman,
  One of the present time.

If apoplexy ever choked in passion's mien, 'twas when
That elderly, and eminent, and honored citizen,

With cheeks empurpled by his wrath, and cuff
pushed back from wrist,
Unable to get out a word, just shook a frantic
fist
    At a polished legal gentleman,
      One of the present time!

"What means such brutal violence?" is counsel's
shrill retort.
"For its protection I appeal to this insulted
court!"
And, skipping back a step or two, in innocent
surprise,
On judge and auditors, he rolls his deprecating
eyes,
    Like a polished legal gentleman,
      One of the present time.

"The case is closed!" proclaims the bench.
    "No more we wish of this;
And for defendant we decide, who's done no
thing amiss."

Then speaks again that lawyer bland, of great
    a-bil-ity :
"We bow, your honor, as we should, unto the
    court's decree—"
    Like a polished legal gentleman,
        One of the present time.

" But, ere we part, I would withdraw whatever
    may reflect
On Mr. Knickerbocker here, who has my high
    respect;
And what I've said implying that his daughter
    is disgraced,
I move may, from the record, be immediately
    erased,"
    Says a polished legal gentleman,
        One of the present time.

Then shakes he hands with all who will; nor
    seems a mite to care,
That Mr. Knickerbocker but salutes him with a
    stare;

And whispering to his client glum, " It's take appeal we will ! "
He hurries to his office to—make out his little bill,
>> Like a polished legal gentleman,
>> One of the present time.

SQUIBS FOR "THE FOURTH."

    Little Jack Horner
    Sat in a corner,
The lock of his pistol to try;
    Down the hammer did come,
    And it blew off his thumb;
Which accounts for his mother's "Oh, my!"

    Ding, dong bell!
    The house is blazing well,
From the crackers Johnny threw upon the roof;
    And from payment might be free,
    The insurance company,
Could they give of Johnny's playfulness the proof.

Druggist, druggist, have you any lint?
Yes, sir, yes, sir; serve you in a min't!
Baby Jones's cannon went off before he thought,
And just above the instep the ramrod has me caught.

Tom, Tim and Bobby were gentlemen wee,
They laid in their beds till the clock struck three;
Then stole out of doors with squib, powder, and gun,
And the sick neighbor died at the rise of the sun.

  Sammy had a Derringer,
  Its barrel black as sloe,
  And when the Derringer went off,
  Did Sammy's hand, also.

Little Bopeep has lost his sleep,
 Since gunpowder quite undermined him;
The matches got lit, in the pocket with it,
 And burned most intensely behind him.

Rocket buy baby, for the housetop,
Point at a stable, and then let it drop;
When the stick breaks the rocket will fall—
Up burn the stable, the horses and all.

Squibs for "The Fourth."

Say, Roman-candle ball, where are you going,
  That the frame cottage so close you illume?
I am a-going, says Roman-candle ball,
  Into that open, third-story back room.

Sing a song of sixpence, the fourth day of July,
A package of torpedoes, with one to hit your eye;
When the lid is opened no pupil there is seen,
And you will wear, until you die, a little shade of green.

THE THIRD TERMAGANT.

1875.

DOMESTIC DETAILS WITH POLITICAL PARALLELS.

WHEN Mr. Redde, the widower, at first came courting me,
I'd no more thought of marrying than jumping in the sea,
An honorable competence and place in life were mine,
And I was happy in my lot, nor tempted to repine.

But he must have a wife, they said,—and who so fit as I
To keep his home in order trim, that all should satisfy?
Full many would no doubt be glad to gain so rich a prize,
Yet none could be compared with me for favor in his eyes.

In short, it seemed, society, with scarce dissenting voice,
Would have me see my duty in consenting to its choice;
Until, at some self-sacrifice, I let them have their way,
And to the union pledged myself—to honor and obey.

I didn't undertake to be perfection, in the bond,
Nor promise what at last might prove all human pow'r beyond;
But readily and cheerfully agreed to do my best,
And leave the hand of Providence to work out all the rest.

Not pausing here to dwell upon the private life we led—
Which surely brought no grave mishap to him whom I had wed—
I'll pass at once to what befell because I would not be
The slave of this and that desire of mixed society.

Because I chose, in quietness, to mind my own
    affairs,
First one and then another dáme thought I was
    taking airs;
From lip to lip the murmur grew, and since I'd
    not reply,
Their gossip swelled to calumny, malevolent and
    high.

My husband sickened presently and died; and
    then 'twas said,
I'd boldly planned to wed again before the man
    was dead!
A partner in his business they mentioned in their
    spleen,
Like brother to poor Mr. Redde—'tis Mr. Whyte
    I mean.

You'd scarce believe the bitter things, revengeful
    and untrue,
That many of my former friends remarked
    about us two;

How Mrs. Bowles and Mrs. Reid, and Mrs. Horace White,
And Mrs. Murat Halstead, too, reviled with all their might.

Combining with my older foe, Miss Nancy Marble called,
They cried, "Another partner's doomed by her to be enthralled!"
Then clamored scandal ev'rywhere, and pitilessly made
A poor old lady challenge me, in rivalry arrayed!

The persecution thus my fate could leave me naught to choose,
And wooed indeed by Mr. Whyte, I did not him refuse.
"You'll have the credit otherwise of wanting me in vain,"
He frankly said. I knew 'twas true—and so I wed again.

There's nothing easier on earth for malice to achieve,
Than talking into being that at which it feigns to grieve;
The busy meddlers I have named, by envy sheer and hate,
Thus badgered me a second time into the marriage state.

And being thus in bonds once more, I strove—am striving still—
To do my duty honestly, with ready hand and will;
Not always free from some mistake—as who that's human is?—
I'm loyal to my husband's rule, to serve the law that's his.

But even while he's yet in life, without a word from me,
Those women I have spoken of have the audacity—

The Third Termagant.

Old Mrs. Bowles, and Mrs. Reid, and Mrs. Bennett, too,
To say I've set my cap to catch a third one—
Mr. Blugh!

The force of envious enmity can hardly further go;
And all because I'll not descend to answer "Yes" or "No!"
Already I've by wiles entrapped two members of the firm,
And must, of course, be scheming for a third connubial term!

It was not of my own free will I first a wife became;
They drove me to the second match to vindicate my name;
And now that Redde and Whyte I've been—the last, indeed, am yet—
The final member of the firm they think I'd die to get.

No thought have I of Mr. Blugh, as well they
    know. But should
They goad me still, I may go mad, as any mortal
    would;
And in the end, if that's the case, their envy,
    spleen and cant,
May make of me, despite myself, a rash Third
    Termagant.

THE SLEIGHING OF OLD.

You may boast as you please of your present Broadway,
With its thunder of wheels through the whole winter's day;
Whence the snow, once the season's chief grace and delight,
Must be carted away, like some pestilent blight,
That the carriage, the 'bus and the wagon of hire
May go lumbering yet upon hub, spoke and tire,
With no sight to the eye and no sound to the ear
Of a change from the stoniest time of the year;—
But to one who remembers how diff'rent the scene
When old Winter's white cloak its gay garment has been,
It is only a skeleton, naked and cold,
Of the brilliant Broadway of the winters of old.

Not so many years, either, have passed since the time
When our Christmas came in to the silvery chime
Of the bells that from thence should as jubilant ring
To the steps of the steed till the coming of spring;
And the street of the city's imperial pride
With the open highway of the countryman vied
In its splendor of fleecy, prismatical white,
Coming down, its bleak pave to transform, in a night.
What a vandal were he who had breathed but the thought
That to cart it away prosy aldermen ought!
Had he spoken the treason, by boyhood's disdain
And a million of snowballs the man had been slain!
But as well might one think of dry-mopping the sea;
For the snows in those days were of polar degree,

The Sleighing of Old.

And ere one had found thaw into trickle and drop.
There was always another to settle on top.

'Twas a bridal of joy for transfigured Broadway,
Thus bedraped, as it were, in a wedding array;
'Twas a signal for something prosaic in life,
For its ploddings of care and its business strife,
To give way for a time to the merrier side
That a true human nature strives vainly to hide.

And, as though they were not, passed the wheels with their roar,
From the scene they had rendered unsightly before;
But to leave in their places bright flashes of steel,
Ever following fast at the horse's quick heel,
And a burden, or greater, or lesser, to bear,
With no sound but the music of bells in the air.

All New York went on runners—went wild on them, too!
From the thoroughbred's driver to him of the screw;

Not a carter so poor but his sled he possessed,
Not a Crœsus so rich that the rule be transgressed;
And the craft upon axletrees showing that day,
Was excluded in scorn from all-sleighing Broadway.

In your fanciful park, on your boulevards wide,
You may think it genteelest of pleasures to ride,
Having sent up your sleigh by express, to be there,
When you ride up yourself in some wheeling affair!
But, not forty years since, the young buck in a sleigh
Who had called it a ride without doing Broadway,
Would have passed for the veriest milksop alive,
And been asked, how it was he was trusted to drive.

Take a sleighride, in sooth, in New York, and not see
Just how merry on runners by daylight 't could be?

The Sleighing of Old.

Take a sleighride by moonlight that was not begun
By essaying Broadway's merry gauntlet to run—
To be pelted with balls and be tooted by horn
On the lofty stage-sleigh and by box-sledder borne?
Take a sleighride, indeed!—Better frankly come down,
And confess it a mere, stupid trip out of town.

Not in all that your fast, fancy avenues show
Of your shoddy and speed on a handful of snow,
Is there anything rife with such good, honest glee,
As a ride behind bells on the road used to be,
When the cutter's keen edge threw out sparks in the cold,
As it flew through Broadway in the sleighing of old.

BEAUTY AND BOOTY.

'Tis of a fair damsel your troubadour sings,
Whose pa was more rich than some old-fashioned
    kings;
A Murray Hill mansion the family owned,
And all their belongings were very high-toned.

Chorus.

*Deftly explaining the perfectly practicable process of reaching
    aristocratic circles without coming of old stock :—*

If money you've made in the fishmonger's line,
Just go into stocks—of a railroad or mine;
And, should the said venture not make you
    repent,
A new airy-stock-racy you'll represent.

This damsel in question was stylishly bred,
And dressed in the mode, from her heels to her
    head;
Yet ever she sighed, as she looked in the glass:
"I'm still only like other maidens, alas!"

Chorus.

Revealing, in strictest confidence, a delicate secret of the ingenuous girlish heart :—

The young female nature is never resigned
To being just like other things of its kind;
But craves some distinction all others above,
If only by one button more on a glove.

At length, as she pondered, a smile wreathed her lip—
"They are still wearing pockets far round on the hip;
I'll have a sacque made on a plan of my own,
With pocket placed somewhere along the backbone!"

Chorus.

Correcting a common mistake of some too careless masculine observers who are utterly unworthy of woman's true affection :—

There bachelors are who indulge the caprice,
That damsels of fashion are all of a piece;

But let the fair creatures despise such attacks,
While diff'rence they have in the cuts of their sacques.

The article ordered came home ere she dined,
And there was the pocket, exactly behind;
She dressed, and put in it a pocket-book's wealth,
Then started out-doors on a walk for her health.

CHORUS.

Showing how an afternoon's airing, under these circumstances, conduces to the health of a maiden of the epoch:—

If, gliding along on a much-crowded street,
The ladies look back at one lady they meet,
Be sure that the one whom thus each eye devours
Feels, therefrom, the better for twenty-four hours.

Our damsel so fair, with the pocket on spine,
Exulted o'er all of her rivals to shine;
But when she was back, and the promenade done,
She found that her pocket-book wealthy—was gone!

CHORUS.

Digressing, for a moment, to a recent remarkable judicial expression of opinion :—

Judge Gildersleeve lately remarked, from the bench,
He didn't design on the fashions to trench;—
But really, as some ladies' pockets are worn,
He wondered more men were not pickpockets born.

The anguish she felt for her money was sore,—
Until her dear pa kindly gave her some more;
Then sought she a jeweler's, straight, with some bonds,
And ordered a set of his best di-a-monds.

CHORUS.

Doing but justice to a really deep and clever device of feminine judgment :—

" If money in cash or in bonds," reasoned she,
" So easily stolen, in daylight, may be,
Much better it is to invest, I declare,
In what, to make sure it is safe, you can wear."

Once more on the avenue's pavement she walked,
While crowds, in her wake, of her jewelry talked;—
An arm round her neck choked down even a cough,
And then, with her diamonds, the scoundrel was off!

Chorus.

Frankly conceding that it is possible for such things to happen in a civilized country:—

When thronged with all sorts of a great city's pop-
Ulation, a street's not as safe as a shop
For showing a fortune in gems, and 'tis prob-
Able that so doing may tempt men to rob.

Our damsel so fair shortly after expired,
Observing: "Of life I'm disgusted and tired!"
And all her dear friends said they thought it was plain,
She'd died of a long-standing soft'ning of brain.

CHORUS.

In which the medical faculty, after scientific investigation, conclude that—! ! !—? ? ?—

But when a post-mortem this story procured,
The poor damsel's parents the doctors assured,
They'd opened her skull, as a final resort,
And found—no foundation for such a report!

NOTES.

NOTES.

1—PAGE 44.

> O'er him bowed the king, and said:
> He is here—and he is dead?

In the realm of intellect it is sometimes given the masses and their viceroys to recognize and reward spontaneous individual excellence; and yet there must be those great ones for whom the eye of majesty alone holds the recognition—coming not until the mortal changes into immortality.

2—PAGE 85.

> 'Tis but when all the nation goes,
> Find leisure to be there he can,
> And never else—which merely show;
> He's only an American.

The local political insignificance of a mere American in New York, is undoubtedly attributable, measurably, to that once-respected citizen's too frequent abstinence from his duty at the polls, save upon occasions of exciting national importance. Thus the great mass of resident foreign statesmen find it incumbent upon them, almost exclusively, to select and elect legislators, mayors, aldermen, and other city officers; and hence the naturally predominant flavor of hod and beer-glass in the manners of the average official representative of the Empire City.

3—PAGE 98.

Then upward winging through the ether, fleet,
  With arms enclasped, arose the shining Three;
  But ever, fading, looking back to Thee,
Thou Shade Eternal, bowing at the feet.

Life at the purest leads but to a grave at which some just accusation, or reproach, might be spoken, and the noblest death that man can die must ever take some tender grace from the Fourth Spirit at the tomb—veiled Silence!

4—PAGE 101.

Now joy to Barbarossa,
  Upon this April day,
When German landsmen hold the lines
  Of Bow'ry and Broadway.

The occupation of New York city by the Germans on the 10th of April, 1871, was not only in celebration of the recent somewhat similar occupation of Paris by the victorious hosts of their good old Kaiser, but also in casual demonstration of their numerical equality, as voters, with the vast Hibernian throng which had taken summary possession of all the leading thoroughfares on the preceding St. Patrick's day. The ensuing bankruptcy of a person of no particular account, as related in the ballad, was a fitting reward for his disrespect in not observing the momentous occasion as a National holiday.

5—PAGE 107.

So, let the rescued city say we fired without command and blund'red;
They take from Providence the word who fifty slay to save five hundred!"

At a critical moment in the "Orange procession" riot, in New York, on July 12th, 1871, the State militia, guarding the marching "Orangemen," became flurried by the ominously-increasing aggression of the surrounding mob, and some of them fired (as was said) "without orders." The moment was that in which many thousands of the rioters, pressing fiercely upon the troops on either side, were just at that pitch of emboldened ferocity when but a trifle might have precipitated their overwhelming onslaught; and the timely volley bringing about fifty of them to the dust—whether delivered by official command or not—certainly turned the scale of what might have become, in another instant, a terribly sanguinary and doubtful battle.

6—PAGE 172.

> Outside assistance is
> Of him the scorn,
> Gentlemen, gentlemen,
> Who's Boston-born!!

It was characteristic of the tremendously high spirit and ineffable solidity of Boston, that, after the great fire in that city, on November 9th, 1872, when the local authorities proposed to receive contributions from other towns for the poorer sufferers, there was much indignation at the idea amongst some of the citizens, who, by notes to the newspapers, protested that Boston was yet rich enough to take care of her own without "outside assistance!"

7—PAGE 173.

> Since Will M. Carleton made us the talk so far and wide,
> There's been no end of town-folks for summer-board applied.

When Mr. Carleton's earliest farm-ballad, "Betsy and I are Out," appeared obscurely in a provincial newspaper, it was the pleasant fortune of the present writer to transplant it promptly to appreciative metropolitan print, with such earnest commendatory notice as assuredly did not detract from its subsequent wide popularity. It was a happy thought to set the practical sentiment of American farm-life to homely, yet dramatically-effective, verse, and this and the succeeding ballads of the series form a volume as characteristically and creditably American as any literary production of the time. Nevertheless, there is a side to agricultural character in the United States not much shown in Mr. Carleton's vigorous verse, and to this the legend of "Chicken and Eggs" is designed to do justice. Ingenuous as our native farmer may be in many of his ways, he is also capable of giving you country-board, selling you a horse, or conveying to you the fee simple of eligible supposititious railroad property in the West, with a degree of acute self-protection not readily to be reconciled with an Arcadian ideal of rustic simplicity. A brace of parodies upon Mr. Carleton's muse may illustrate this proposition:

"BETSY AND I ARE OUT."

Go 'tend the door, there, Bridget, and mind what you're about,
For Betsy's mother's comin', and Betsy and I are out;
I've stood the dear old lady as long as ever I can,
And the more I've tried to stan' it, the more I've had to stan'.

Since first we two got married, and came down here to live,
She's had no end of orders and free advice to give;
There's nothin' a hand is put to, outside of the house or in,
But she has a say about it that's always sure to win.

From nursin' babies to cleanin', from hayin' to milkin' cows,
We've give her her way entirely, as much as the law allows;
There's hardly a child or critter, a field, or a fence, or stone,
She hasn't a fault to find with, or ever can leave alone.

Perhaps I might stan' *that* much, if Betsy so should bid,
And let the old lady boss it the same as she always did;
But now that her tongue has taken to waggin' another course,
I've got to be up an' doin', or look for a cheap divorce.

If I but say she's a-meddlin', she tells my wife I drink;
If ever I look at a woman, she gives my wife the wink;
And comin' from meetin', Sunday, when Betsy was taken ill,
She said, that for half the symptoms, a woman could file a bill!

So, 'tend the door, there, Bridget, and keep your wits about,
And tell the dear old lady that Betsy and I are out;
And then—in case she threatens to come some other day—
Just add to the statement, Bridget, that out we intend to stay?

"OUT OF THE OLD HOUSE, NANCY."

Out of the old house, Nancy—movin' at last, you see.
And up in the new one, yonder, shall settled quickly be;
But not for a good ten minutes the stage we take goes by,
So there's no need for hurry, nor bein' quite so spry.

The first day that we came here was that on which we wed,
When many a one was livin' that now is cold and dead;
The very door we entered is green with the old paint still,
And the same old chany-asters are growing by the sill.

Up in the room that's whitewashed, we heard our Tom's first cry,
And down in the room that's papered we saw our Mary die;
There ain't a thing in the homestead but's breathin' with our breath,
There ain't a stairway in it but's long as life and death.

There ain't a turn nor a corner but's holding for us still,
What don't come out with the fixin's—what don't and never will;
We've cleared our duds to the leastmost, from carpet-tack to blind,
But there's more than them there, Nancy, which we must leave behind.

There's laughs for good old doin's, there's tears for troubles shared,
That stay in the walls and floorin' the more that they are bared;
We can't take *them* off with us, however we may try,
No more than the undertaker our spirits when we die.

I thought that the p'int was settled, that here we'd always stay,
Until that chap from Eastward came pryin' round this way,
And said he thought of takin' a farm and a house out West,
And asked my frank opinion of what to buy was best.

Seein' he had the money; seein' he'd caught the tune
Of makin' a Western fortin', as whistled by the *Tribune*,
I kind 'f let on, unconscious, that *this* was a place for sale,
Which couldn't be bought for *no* price when railroads should prevail.

And when he asked if a railroad was like "*this* way" to fork,
I said that more than one would come in "*this* way" from New York;
For this from 'York is west'ard, and what comes west from there
Can't help but come out "*this* way" *some distance*, I could swear!

The way he snapt at the bargain, and closed it, after that,
Was 'though I'd offered a gold mine—it came so strong and pat.
He gave me my own price for it, and seemed like all aflame
To be th' old farm's possessor, in full, when the railroad came!

Out of the old house, Nancy, we move to one that's new,
To hold our heads with the great folks, once scornin' me an' you;
'Tis good to stick to the old place until you have the luck
To sell to a down-east Yankee, who then, in turn, is "stuck!"

www.ingramcontent.com/pod-product-compliance
Lightning Source LLC
Chambersburg PA
CBHW021831230426
43669CB00008B/931